The CHOSEN

SEASON THREE

KIDS ACTIVITY BOOK

BroadStreet
KIDS

BroadStreet Kids
Savage, Minnesota, USA

BroadStreet Kids is an imprint of BroadStreet Publishing®
Broadstreetpublishing.com

The
CHOSEN

Kids Activity Book: Season 3
© 2024 by The Chosen LLC

978-1-4245-6489-7

Design by Chris Garborg | garborgdesign.com
Created, edited, and compiled by Michelle Winger | literallyprecise.com
Mazes licensed from mazegenerator.net.

Printed in China.

24 25 26 27 28 29 30   7 6 5 4 3 2 1

Alphabet practice!

Practice the first three letters of the Hebrew alphabet!

ALEF

This Hebrew letter is silent.

BET

This letter sounds like the **b** in boat.

GIMEL

This letter sounds like the **g** in goat.

PRETTY POTS

USE THE LETTERS AND NUMBERS
TO SHOW WHERE EACH OF THESE
PIECES BELONG IN THE PUZZLE.
WE GOT YOU STARTED! ⟶  C8

_____

_____

_____

_____

_____

_____

_____

_____

Answer on page 150

SECRET DECODER

Use the code to decipher the words Jesus spoke to His disciples (in Luke 12:22-25) about being anxious.

Use the blue numbers from the first puzzle to complete the phrase in the second box.

※	◆	●	✦	⌘	🐟	◈	💧	▲	✝	◎	🕯	⚡
A	B	C	D	E	F	G	H	I	J	K	L	M

🔑	♫	☐	✖	💰	❄	🌧	☸	★	☼	❀	✡	❖
N	O	P	Q	R	S	T	U	V	W	X	Y	Z

NUMBER

Jesus talked about considering our own actions before we say that other people are wrong (Matthew 7:1-3).

Use the grid to figure out which letters go where, so you can read His advice. We have given you some numbers to start.

A	B	C	D	E	F	G	H	I	J	K	L	M
										16		

N	O	P	Q	R	S	T	U	V	W	X	Y	Z
11	22		17		8	13	24		15		23

CODE

$\overline{6}$ $\overline{13}$ $\overline{25}$ $\overline{14}$ $\overline{12}$ $\overline{11}$ $\overline{22}$ $\overline{8}$ $\overline{8}$ $\overline{26}$ $\overline{9}$ $\overline{8}$ $\overline{19}$ $\overline{22}$ $\overline{13}$

$\overline{11}$ $\overline{22}$ $\overline{8}$ $\overline{18}$ $\overline{12}$ $\overline{6}$ $\overline{13}$ $\overline{25}$ $\overline{14}$ $\overline{12}$ $\overline{25}$ $\overline{2}$ $\overline{22}$ $\overline{5}$

$\overline{7}$ $\overline{3}$ $\overline{8}$ $\overline{26}$ $\overline{8}$ $\overline{26}$ $\overline{12}$ $\overline{6}$ $\overline{13}$ $\overline{25}$ $\overline{14}$ $\overline{21}$ $\overline{12}$ $\overline{11}$ $\overline{8}$

$\overline{19}$ $\overline{22}$ $\overline{13}$ $\overline{1}$ $\overline{5}$ $\overline{22}$ $\overline{11}$ $\overline{22}$ $\overline{13}$ $\overline{11}$ $\overline{4}$ $\overline{12}$ $\overline{19}$ $\overline{22}$ $\overline{13}$

$\overline{7}$ $\overline{3}$ $\overline{10}$ $\overline{10}$ $\overline{18}$ $\overline{12}$ $\overline{6}$ $\overline{13}$ $\overline{25}$ $\overline{14}$ $\overline{12}$ $\overline{25}$' $\overline{9}$ $\overline{11}$ $\overline{25}$

$\overline{7}$ $\overline{3}$ $\overline{8}$ $\overline{26}$ $\overline{8}$ $\overline{26}$ $\overline{12}$ $\overline{21}$ $\overline{12}$ $\overline{9}$ $\overline{20}$ $\overline{13}$ $\overline{5}$ $\overline{12}$

$\overline{19}$ $\overline{22}$ $\overline{13}$ $\overline{13}$ $\overline{20}$ $\overline{12}$ $\overline{3}$ $\overline{8}$ $\overline{7}$ $\overline{3}$ $\overline{10}$ $\overline{10}$ $\overline{18}$ $\overline{12}$

$\overline{21}$ $\overline{12}$ $\overline{9}$ $\overline{20}$ $\overline{13}$ $\overline{5}$ $\overline{12}$ $\overline{25}$ $\overline{8}$ $\overline{22}$ $\overline{19}$ $\overline{22}$ $\overline{13}$

Word Search

Find the characters hidden in the word search puzzle.

ANDREW

BIG JAMES

EDEN

JESUS

JOHN

JUDAS

LITTLE JAMES

MARY MAGDALENE

MATTHEW

NATHANAEL

PHILIP

RAMAH

SIMON

TAMAR

THADDEUS

THOMAS

ZEE

```
                    B
                    V
                    E   T
                B   H   B   S
            K   A   L   I   A   Y
            D   I   T   G   M   N   H
        D   J   P   S   J   O   W   Y
        E   Z   V   R   U   A   H   G   E   A
    U   Y   P   A   F   S   M   T   S   J   R   T
  S   K   O   M   U   Z   E   E   R   U   I   O   D   G
  L   W   A   Z   X   F   J   S   D   H   X   M   I   N   P
C   L   T   A   G   X   I   H   A   M   A   R   L   O   F   A   W
O   V   I   V   E   C   W   Z   S   W   T   C   Q   U   D   N   L   E
U   M   A   T   T   H   E   W   S   E   M   A   J   E   L   T   T   I   L   N
                    H
                    O
L   A   O   N   Y   W   D   Z   T   U   V   P   I   L   I   H   P   U   Y   E
Y   U   H   E   N   E   L   A   D   G   A   M   Y   R   A   M   Y   D
G   O   E   E   K   I   M   C   V   O   N   J   T   U   N   E
J   L   E   A   N   A   H   T   A   N   Y   N   K   N
```

WHICH FISH?

Each colored fish in the puzzle represents a letter (all five vowels and two consonants). Figure out which fish carries which letter, and then read what Jesus said in Matthew 6:32-33 about the things of the world.

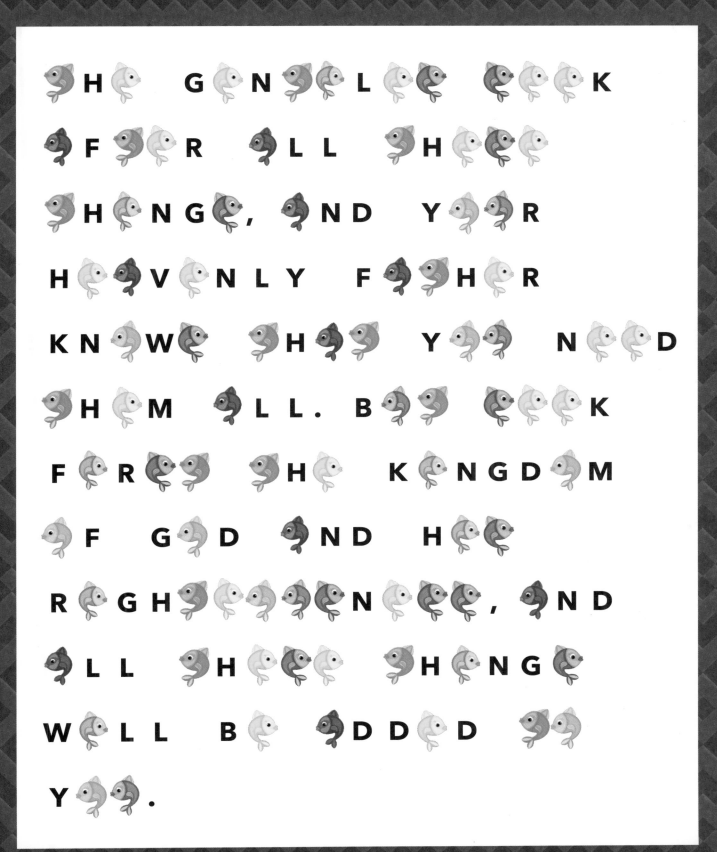

Answer on page 150

WORD FIT

The names of some places seen or talked about in Season 3 only fit into the puzzle one way. Use the number of letters in each word as a clue to where it could be put. We have placed a word to help you get started.

4 LETTERS
ROME

5 LETTERS
JOPPA
NAVEH
PEREA

6 LETTERS
SHARON
TELDOR

7 LETTERS
JERICHO
KERIOTH
SAMARIA

8 LETTERS
NAZARETH

9 LETTERS
CAPERNAUM
DECAPOLIS
JERUSALEM
MACHAERUS
PTOLEMAIS
SEPPHORIS

14 LETTERS
KORAZIM PLATEAU

16 LETTERS
CAESAREA PHILIPPI

Answer on page 150

PATH WORDS

Beginning with the yellow star and ending with the red stop sign, connect the people to re-create some of Jesus' words found in Matthew 7:12. (Hint: this is usually what we call "The Golden Rule.")

Each person must be visited once and only once, and they have to be connected using the paths (side-to-side and up-and-down).

Write the missing words here as you go along.

WHATEVER _____ _____

_____ _____ _____

_____ _____ YOU _____

_____ _____ _____,

FOR _____ _____

_____ _____ _____

_____ PROPHETS.

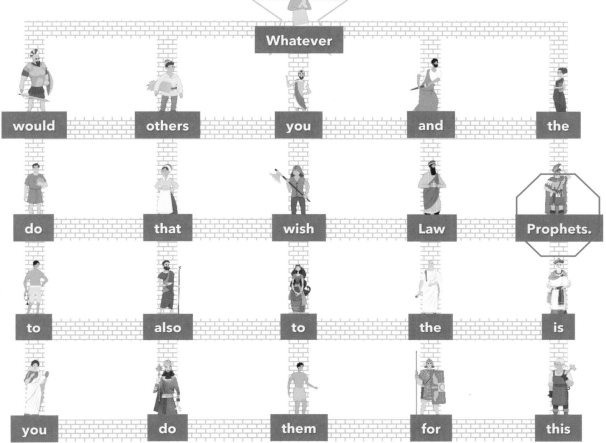

Answer on page 151

BIRD WORDS

Each of the trees have enough birds holding letters to spell one word. Match the trees with the crates of seeds to figure out which set of letters belongs where. Then, unscramble the letters and write the word in the spaces under each crate. When you are done, you will be able to read what Jesus said in Matthew 6:25-26 about taking care of you.

IS NOT _ _ _ _ _   MORE THAN _ _ _ _ _ ,

AND THE _ _ _ _ _   MORE THAN _ _ _ _ _ _ _ _ _ _ ?

LOOK AT THE _ _ _ _ _ _   OF THE _ _ _ :   THEY NEITHER _ _ _

NOR _ _ _ _ _   NOR GATHER INTO _ _ _ _ _ _ ,   AND YET

YOUR _ _ _ _ _ _ _ _ _ _ _   FATHER _ _ _ _ _ _ THEM.

ARE YOU NOT OF MORE _ _ _ _ _ _ THAN THEY?

JUMBLED WORDS

In Matthew 6:9-13, Jesus taught His disciples how to pray.

Unscramble the words so you can read *The Lord's Prayer*.

R U O   H A F E R T   N I

E V A E H N   L O L A H E W D

E B   U Y O R   A E M N .

U O R Y   G D K O I M N

M E C O '   U O R Y   L I W L

E B   N O D E   N O   R E T A H

S A   T I   S I   N I

E̅ A̅ E̅ V̅ H̅ N̅ . V̅ I̅ G̅ E̅   S̅ U̅

H̅ I̅ T̅ S̅   Y̅ A̅ D̅   U̅ R̅ O̅

A̅ Y̅ I̅ D̅ L̅   R̅ A̅ D̅ E̅ B̅ ' N̅ A̅ D̅

R̅ F̅ O̅ I̅ V̅ E̅ G̅   S̅ U̅   U̅ R̅ O̅

B̅ T̅ E̅ D̅ S̅ ' S̅ A̅   E̅ W̅   S̅ O̅ A̅ L̅

V̅ E̅ A̅ H̅   R̅ O̅ F̅ I̅ G̅ N̅ E̅ V̅

U̅ O̅ R̅   D̅ T̅ B̅ R̅ O̅ S̅ E̅ .   D̅ N̅ A̅

E̅ A̅ L̅ D̅   S̅ U̅   O̅ T̅ N̅   T̅ N̅ O̅ I̅

N̅ E̅ P̅ T̅ A̅ T̅ M̅ I̅ T̅ O̅ ' T̅ U̅ B̅

V̅ E̅ D̅ L̅ I̅ R̅ E̅   S̅ U̅   M̅ O̅ R̅ F̅

L̅ I̅ V̅ E̅ .

Answer on page 151

PICTURE PUZZLE

Use the pictures to help you figure out what Jesus said to His disciples in Matthew 6:19-21 about treasure.

– G　　 – K　　 – H + L　　　　**4** – U

_____　　_____　　_____　　_____

YOURSELVES _____　_____　_____ WHERE

　　**&**　　 　　**&**

_____　_____ DESTROY _____ WHERE

　　　　　　**&**　　 – K + L

_____　_____　_____　_____ .

 – H + L　　　　**4** – U　　

_____　_____　_____ YOURSELVES _____

_____　_____ WHERE NEITHER _____ NOR _____

&　　　　 – G　　 – K

DESTROYS _____ WHERE _____　_____　_____

　　　　&　　 – K + L　　**4** – U

_____　_____ . _____ WHERE YOUR

　　　　 – H + W  – E

_____ IS, THERE YOUR _____　_____ ALSO.

Answer on page 151

CAUSE
AND
EFFECT

Jesus told a story about wise and foolish builders in Matthew 7:24-27.

Use the letter tiles to complete the missing parts of the words in each section of the chart.

A vertical line in the middle of the box means there is more than one word in that box.

The colored arrows will help you follow the path to tell each side of the story.

ISH	SE	EY	ON
ST	DIS	HOU	FO
DS	LLS	CK	WI
	OB	SA	

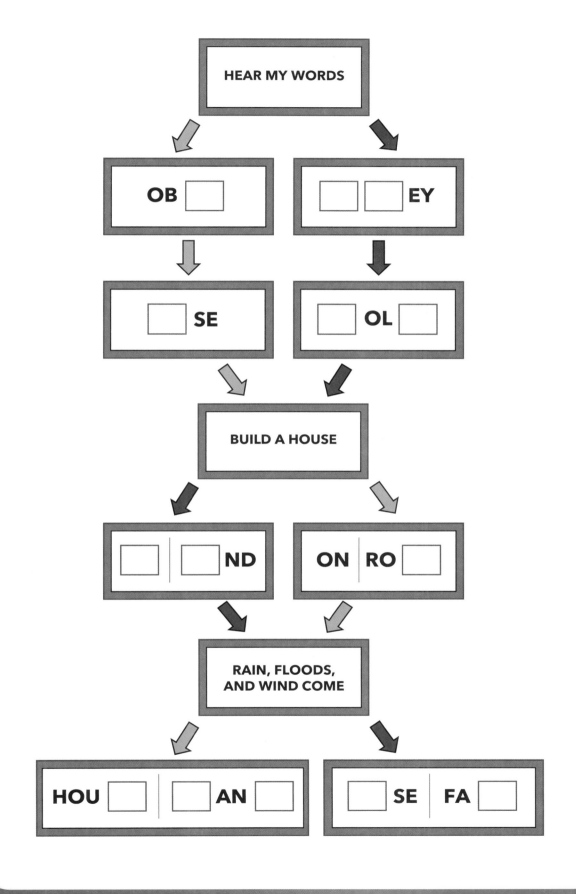

Which Fish?

Each colored fish in the puzzle represents a letter (all five vowels and two consonants). Figure out which fish carries which letter, and then read one of the blessings Jesus prayed over the disciples from Numbers 6:24-26.

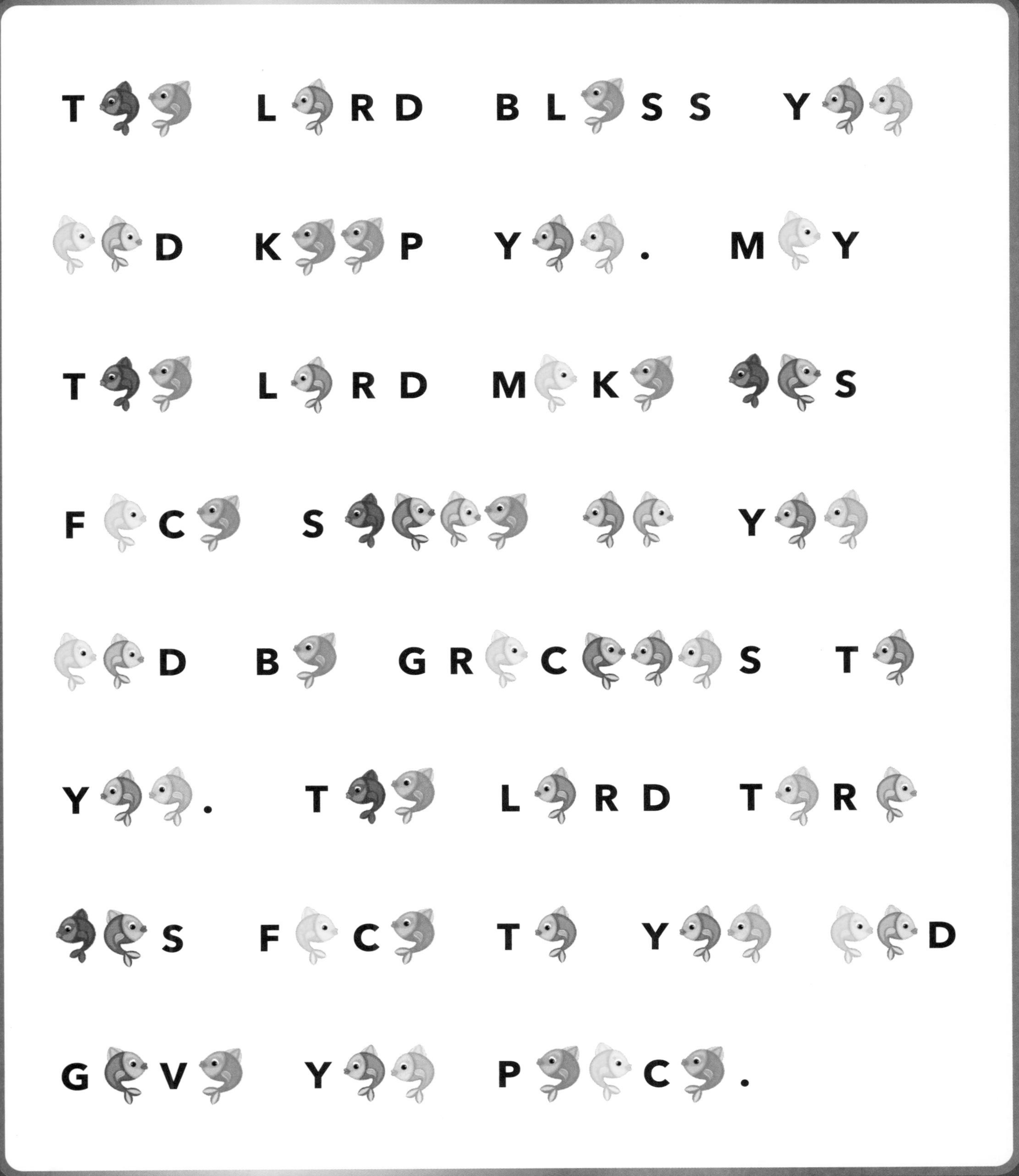

T🐟🐟 L🐟RD BL🐟SS Y🐟🐟

🐟🐟D K🐟🐟P Y🐟🐟. M🐟Y

T🐟🐟 L🐟RD M🐟K🐟 🐟S

F🐟C🐟 S🐟🐟🐟 🐟🐟 Y🐟🐟

🐟🐟D B🐟 GR🐟C🐟🐟S T🐟

Y🐟🐟. T🐟🐟 L🐟RD T🐟R🐟

🐟🐟S F🐟C🐟 T🐟 Y🐟🐟 🐟🐟D

G🐟V🐟 Y🐟🐟 P🐟🐟C🐟.

Answer on page 152

In Matthew 5:23-24, Jesus told the people that if they were offering a gift at the altar and realized they needed to make something right with someone, they should go home and take care of that first, and then come back to the altar.

Beginning at the altar (center of the maze), find your way home and back to the altar without crossing your own path.

Alphabet practice!

Practice the next three letters of the Hebrew alphabet!

DALET

This letter sounds like the **d** in doll.

ד

HE

This letter sounds like the **h** in horse.

ה

WAW

This letter sounds like the **w** in well.

ו

GLITTERY GOLD

USE THE LETTERS AND NUMBERS
TO SHOW WHERE EACH OF THESE
PIECES BELONG IN THE PUZZLE.
WE GOT YOU STARTED! ⟶ <u>E5</u>

_____

_____

_____

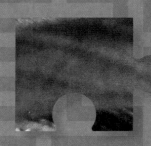

_____

_____

_____

_____

_____

Answer on page 152

Word Search

Find the characters hidden in the word search puzzle.

ALPHAEUS
BARNABY
DASHA
DINAH
DVORAH
ELISHEVA
HADAD
JAIRUS
JOANNA
JOHN THE BAPTIST
JULIUS
LAZARUS
LUCIUS
MARTHA
MARY
MOTHER MARY
NICODEMUS
RAFI
RIVKA
SALOME
SHMUEL
SHULA
ZEBEDEE

```
L M C N F G M M Y P G I S G U B V V A D
W J A R X B M O Y B U U Y E S H U L A J
M O J S U I L U J T I M P L J H H P K L
W H X Y O W N E G C Y E R I C X D G V A
I N F D R V V N U T L D A S H A K Q L Z
F T X V J A Q L S E Y L J H S S C Y A
K H M O W T T F U M I G O E J J T I T R
M E L R Z G P M M A Z X A V X A I N P U
Z B I A W T H K E F C F N A A I I A S S
I A H H R S F K D P U P N R E V G R T E
L P F X Z M Z S O R K S A L O M E S U W
E T F H H O Q U C N M V T U J E Z R H S
M I B F P T Y E I B U F Z A J C H A A A
D S R Q R H R A N X E P A C A D I T N F
S T K X T E E H R A Y X B H S P T A I F
K N E I H R M P N W X S T A R E Y D D D
T M W T F M K L M P R R K X O K C T A F
R I V K A A E A J N A K D P L P K D U D
P W F T F R R T J M L L B A R N A B Y W
L W D S B Y B B Z E B E D E E H C Y V A
```

CROSSWORD FUN

Use the clues to solve the crossword. Answers with two words are shown in parentheses revealing how many letters are in each word.

ACROSS

2. The woman who lost a baby while her husband was on a mission with Jesus

5. The new synagogue administrator

9. Matthew's father

10. The disciple Jesus worked with to write down His sermon

11. The woman Tamar and Ramah went to stay with (4, 9)

DOWN

1. The disciple whose name means "God be praised"

3. The disciple who went to ask Ramah's father for permission to marry her

4. The disciple who admitted to dreaming of his mother's cinnamon cakes every day (3, 5)

5. The woman who gave her shawl as an offering

6. The woman who was healed when she touched Jesus

7. One of the disciples who went to stay with Simon and Eden

8. He sold his fishing boat and started making olive oil instead

12. The rabbi who stored his documents in a locked cellar

13. The disciple who went to visit John the Baptist in jail

WATCH SEASON 3, ESPECIALLY EPISODES 1-2, TO HELP YOU COMPLETE THIS CROSSWORD!

Answer on page 152

SECRET DECODER

Use the code to decipher the words spoken by Jesus (in Episode 2) to His disciples before He sent them out. Use the numbers to complete the other phrase Jesus said to them.

※	◆	●	✦	⌘	🐟	◈	◐	▲	✝	◎	🕯	⚡
A	B	C	D	E	F	G	H	I	J	K	L	M

🔑	♫	☐	✖	💰	❄	🌧	⚙	★	☼	❀	✡	❖
N	O	P	Q	R	S	T	U	V	W	X	Y	Z

38

WORD IN WORD

Use the definitions to figure out the words. The letters in the small words will help you figure out the bigger words.

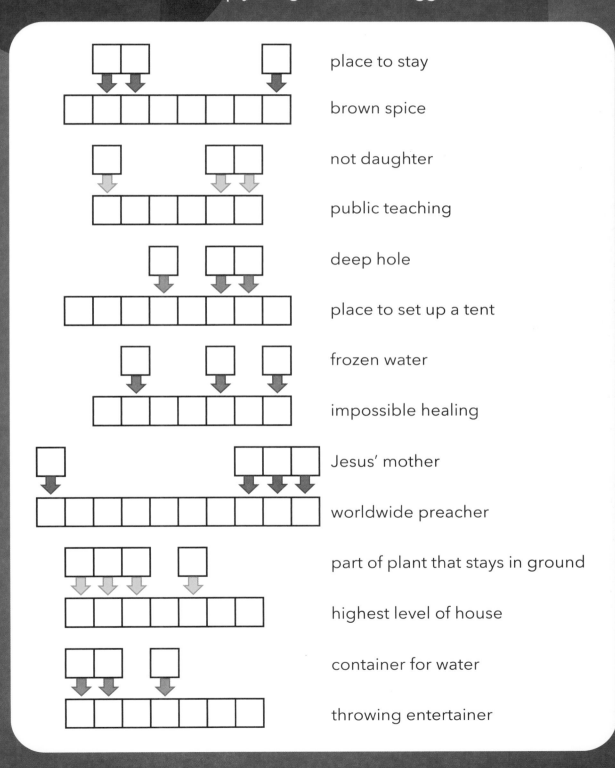

place to stay

brown spice

not daughter

public teaching

deep hole

place to set up a tent

frozen water

impossible healing

Jesus' mother

worldwide preacher

part of plant that stays in ground

highest level of house

container for water

throwing entertainer

Answer on page 152

MAZE

Make your way through the tent village and see how many fires you can put out along the way. You can go through fires to put them out, but you must avoid the tents, and you can't cross the same path twice.

How many fires did you extinguish?

_____

Start here

NUMBER CODE

Jesus gave His disciples something to think about before he sent them on their first mission (from Episode 2).

Use the grid to figure out which letters go where, so you can read what He told them. We have given you some numbers to start.

A	B	C	D	E	F	G	H	I	J	K	L	M
	3						22		26			

N	O	P	Q	R	S	T	U	V	W	X	Y	Z
12			24	1		8	13			23		25

$\overline{18}\ \overline{6}\ \overline{13}\quad \overline{1}\ \overline{7}\ \overline{17}\ \overline{7}\ \overline{2}\ \overline{9}\ \overline{7}\ \overline{11}\quad \overline{14}\ \overline{2}\ \overline{8}\ \overline{22}\ \overline{6}\ \overline{13}\ \overline{8}$

$\overline{4}\ \overline{16}\ \overline{18}\ \overline{2}\ \overline{12}\ \overline{10}\quad ;\quad \overline{12}\ \overline{6}\ \overline{14}\quad \overline{10}\ \overline{2}\ \overline{9}\ \overline{7}$

$\overline{14}\ \overline{2}\ \overline{8}\ \overline{22}\ \overline{6}\ \overline{13}\ \overline{8}\quad \overline{4}\ \overline{16}\ \overline{18}\ .$

$\overline{14}\ \overline{22}\ \overline{16}\ \overline{8}\ \overline{7}\ \overline{9}\ \overline{7}\ \overline{1}\quad \overline{8}\ \overline{6}\ \overline{14}\ \overline{12}\quad \overline{6}\ \overline{1}$

$\overline{9}$ $\overline{2}$ $\overline{19}$ $\overline{19}$ $\overline{16}$ $\overline{10}$ $\overline{7}$ $\overline{18}$ $\overline{6}$ $\overline{13}$ $\overline{7}$ $\overline{12}$ $\overline{8}$ $\overline{7}$ $\overline{1}$ '

$\overline{20}$ $\overline{2}$ $\overline{12}$ $\overline{11}$ $\overline{6}$ $\overline{13}$ $\overline{8}$ $\overline{14}$ $\overline{22}$ $\overline{6}$ $\overline{2}$ $\overline{21}$

$\overline{14}$ $\overline{6}$ $\overline{1}$ $\overline{8}$ $\overline{22}$ $\overline{18}$ $\overline{2}$ $\overline{12}$ $\overline{2}$ $\overline{8}$ $\overline{16}$ $\overline{12}$ $\overline{11}$

$\overline{21}$ $\overline{8}$ $\overline{16}$ $\overline{18}$ $\overline{8}$ $\overline{22}$ $\overline{7}$ $\overline{1}$ $\overline{7}$ $\overline{13}$ $\overline{12}$ $\overline{8}$ $\overline{2}$ $\overline{19}$ $\overline{18}$ $\overline{6}$ $\overline{13}$

$\overline{11}$ $\overline{7}$ $\overline{4}$ $\overline{16}$ $\overline{1}$ $\overline{8}$. $\overline{2}$ $\overline{20}$ $\overline{16}$ $\overline{12}$ $\overline{18}$ $\overline{6}$ $\overline{12}$ $\overline{7}$

$\overline{14}$ $\overline{2}$ $\overline{19}$ $\overline{19}$ $\overline{12}$ $\overline{6}$ $\overline{8}$ $\overline{1}$ $\overline{7}$ $\overline{17}$ $\overline{7}$ $\overline{2}$ $\overline{9}$ $\overline{7}$ $\overline{18}$ $\overline{6}$ $\overline{13}$

$\overline{6}$ $\overline{1}$ $\overline{19}$ $\overline{2}$ $\overline{21}$ $\overline{8}$ $\overline{7}$ $\overline{12}$ $\overline{8}$ $\overline{6}$ $\overline{18}$ $\overline{6}$ $\overline{13}$ $\overline{1}$

$\overline{14}$ $\overline{6}$ $\overline{1}$ $\overline{11}$ $\overline{21}$ ' $\overline{21}$ $\overline{22}$ $\overline{16}$ $\overline{15}$ $\overline{7}$ $\overline{6}$ $\overline{20}$ $\overline{20}$ $\overline{8}$ $\overline{22}$ $\overline{7}$

$\overline{11}$ $\overline{13}$ $\overline{21}$ $\overline{8}$ $\overline{20}$ $\overline{1}$ $\overline{6}$ $\overline{5}$ $\overline{18}$ $\overline{6}$ $\overline{13}$ $\overline{1}$ $\overline{20}$ $\overline{7}$ $\overline{7}$ $\overline{8}$

$\overline{14}$ $\overline{22}$ $\overline{7}$ $\overline{12}$ $\overline{18}$ $\overline{6}$ $\overline{13}$ $\overline{19}$ $\overline{7}$ $\overline{16}$ $\overline{9}$ $\overline{7}$ $\overline{8}$ $\overline{22}$ $\overline{16}$ $\overline{8}$ '

$\overline{22}$ $\overline{6}$ $\overline{13}$ $\overline{21}$ $\overline{7}$ $\overline{6}$ $\overline{1}$ $\overline{8}$ $\overline{6}$ $\overline{14}$ $\overline{12}$ $\overline{11}$ $\overline{6}$ $\overline{12}$ $\overline{8}$

$\overline{14}$ $\overline{16}$ $\overline{21}$ $\overline{8}$ $\overline{7}$ $\overline{18}$ $\overline{6}$ $\overline{13}$ $\overline{1}$ $\overline{8}$ $\overline{2}$ $\overline{5}$ $\overline{7}$

Answer on page 153

LETTER WHEEL

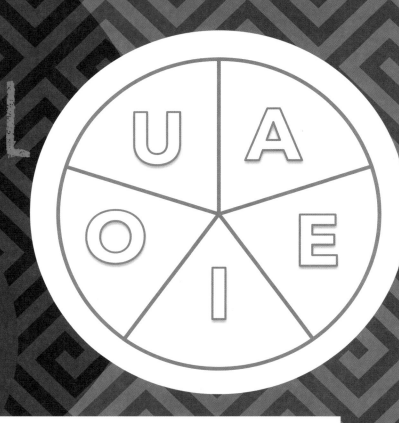

Use the letters in the wheel to complete Jesus' message to Little James (in Episode 2) about his healing. Letters can be used multiple times.

T_ KN_W H_W T_ ST_LL PR__S_
G_D _N SP_T_ _F TH_S, T_
KN_W H_W T_ F_C_S _N _LL
TH_T M_TT_RS S_ M_CH M_R_
TH_N TH_ B_DY. T_ SH_W
P__PL_ H_W Y__ C_N B_
P_T__NT W_TH Y__R S_FF_R_NG

H_R_ _N __RTH B_C_ _S_ Y_ _
KN_W Y_ _'LL SP_ND _T_RN_TY
W_TH N_ S_FF_R_NG. N_T
_V_RY_N_ C_N _ND_RST_ND TH_T.
H_LD _N _ L_TTL_ L_NG_R,
_ND WH_N Y_ _ F_ND TR_ _
STR_NGTH B_C_ _S_ _F Y_ _R
W_ _KN_SS, _ND WH_N Y_ _
D_ GR_ _T TH_NGS _N MY
N_M_ _N SP_T_ _F TH_S,
TH_ _MP_CT W_LL L_ST F_R
G_N_R_T_ _NS.
Y_ _ W_LL B_ H_ _L_D…
_T'S _NLY _ M_TT_R _F T_M_.

Answer on page 153

Word Search

Find the characters hidden in the word search puzzle.

ATTICUS	MACHIR
AUGUR	MARIUS
AVNER	NADAB
CLAUDIA	NASHON
DIMITRIUS	OZEM
EREMIS	PONTIUS
GAIUS	QUINTUS
HEROD	TIBERIUS
JEKAMIAH	YAELI
JOSEPH	YANNI
KAFNI	YUSSIF
LEANDER	

```
                        G   P
                        A   N
S   A                   I           Y   B
R   W                   U   W           A   N
    U   R       F   I   S   S   U   Y       N   W
        G   J   E   K   A   M   I   A   H   N   S
            U   K   S   M   A   C   H   I   R   U
            I   B   A   I   U   C   L   A   U   D   I   A
            S   W   W   M   S   B   J   S   B   J   T   I
L   S   U   I   R   A   M   E   U   Z   U   D   A   P   N   V   B   J   T   L
O   N   A   S   H   O   N   R   I   I   O   Q   D   I   O   O   O   Y   L   P
            U   X   V   E   R   R   C   K   A   H   P   S
            M   C   F   T   E   L   E   A   N   D   E   R
            E   I   H   B   T   Q   F   X   P   A
            M   Z   T   I   L   U   N   H   O   I   V
        I   B       O   T   Y   I   I   I           Y   N
    D   Q                   A   N               V   E
V   I                       E   T               A   R
                            L   U
                            I   S
```

47

CROSSWORD FUN

Use the clues to solve the crossword puzzle. Answers with two words are shown in parentheses revealing how many letters are in each word.

ACROSS

1. The person who gave Jesus the bridle

3. What Jesus said He didn't like in the bread His mother made

5. What Alphaeus gave back to Matthew

6. He was in charge of the women's safety while the disciples were on mission

7. The disciple Matthew said was his friend

9. The disciple who hadn't yet received healing (6, 5)

12. Who Matthew met outside his house

14. The sister of Lazarus whose name wasn't Mary

15. What Jesus when to get from the box in His old room

17. The disciple who was concerned about getting money for the ministry

DOWN

2. What Zebedee decided to start producing and selling (5, 3)

4. The disciple who was concerned about fires being so close to the tents

5. What Jesus took from Zee and threw in the river

8. The type of plant Judas gave to Dvorah to take care of

10. Jesus' childhood friend

11. The disciple who apologized to Mary Magdalene for saying awful things to her

13. Jesus told His mother this disciple was still a bit of a wild animal

16. What was missing from the city gates when Jesus arrived home

WATCH SEASON 3, ESPECIALLY EPISODES 2-3, TO HELP YOU COMPLETE THIS CROSSWORD!

Answer on page 153

MAZE

After the long trip, the followers of Jesus were excited to get home. (Watch Episode Four!) Help each person find their way to the house they would be staying in. There are clues below to help you figure out who goes where.

- o Mary's house is Red.
- o Simon & Eden's house is not Green.
- o Nathanael went to the Blue house.
- o Zee went to Simon & Eden's house, but it was not Yellow.
- o All the women went to Mary's house.
- o Zebedee's house is not Yellow.
- o Simon, Andrew, and John all went to their own homes.
- o Big James and Thomas went to Zebedee's house.
- o Philip went to Andrew's house which was not Green or Blue.

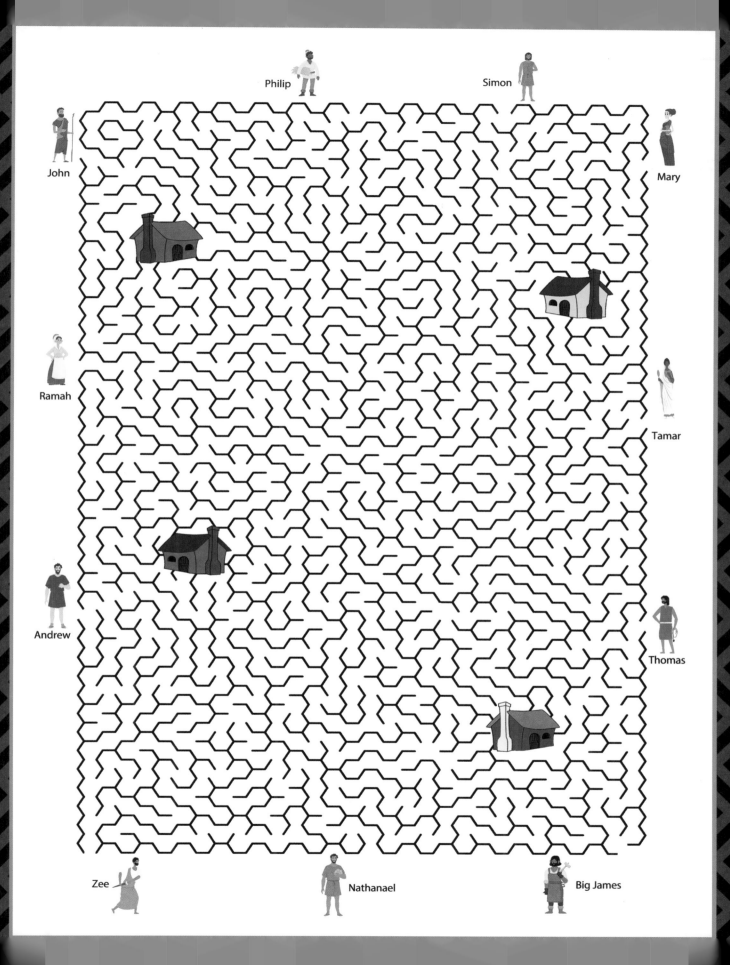

SECRET DECODER

Use the code to decipher the psalm recited by the disciples in Episode 2. Once you've done the first section, use the numbers to complete the second section.

※	◆	●	✦	⌘	🐟	◈	💧	⛰	✝	◎	🕯	⚡
A	B	C	D	E	F	G	H	I	J	K	L	M

🔑	♪	□	✕	💰	❄	🌧	☸	★	☼	❀	✡	❖
N	O	P	Q	R	S	T	U	V	W	X	Y	Z

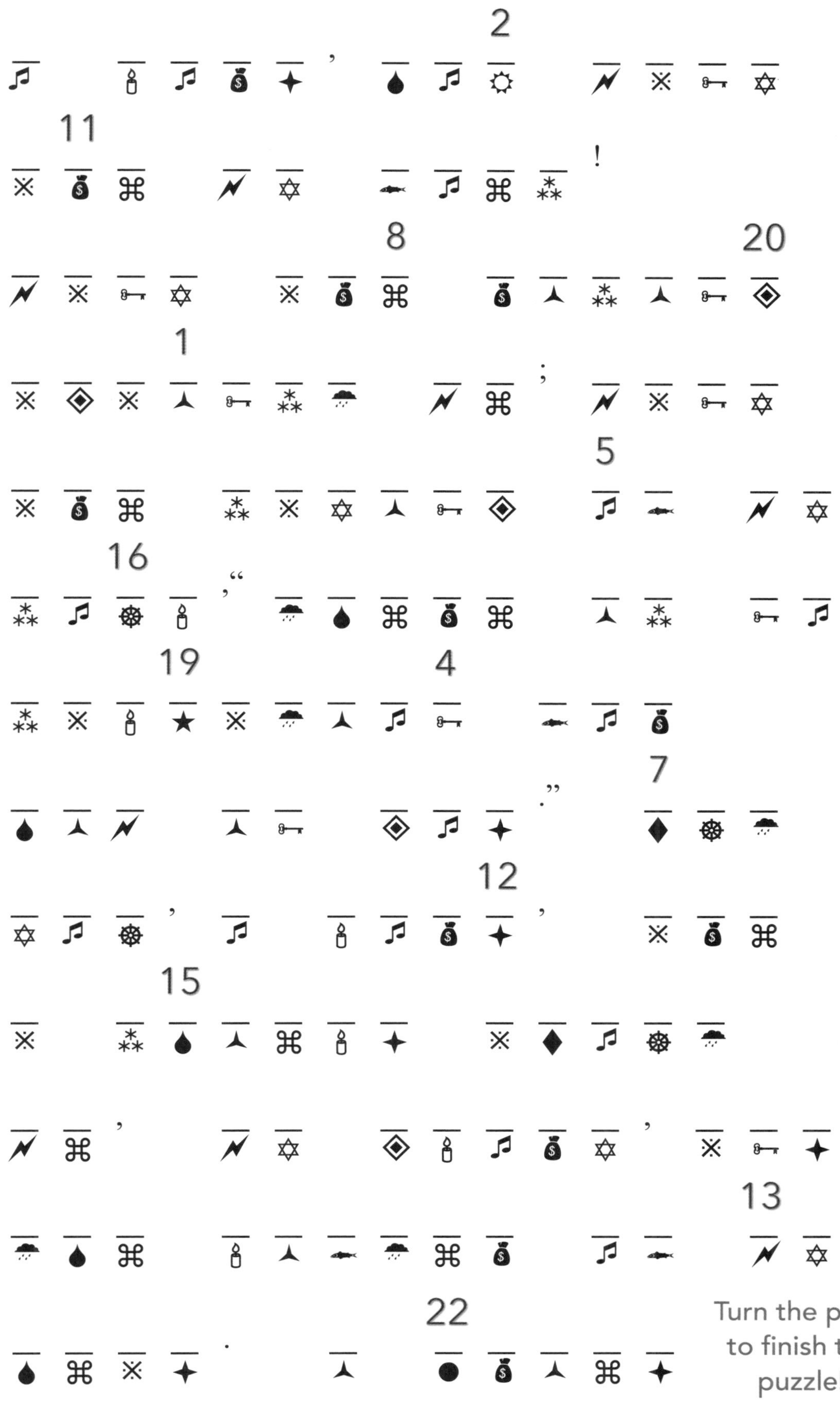

Turn the page to finish the puzzle!

18	8	5	18	3	8		2	15	5		15	9	19	8

17 8 6   6 15 8 13 17 8 3 19 8 17

9 20 9 1 4 17 6   13 8   9 3 3

9 11 5 16 4 12 .   9 11 1 17 8 ,   5

3 5 11 12 !   17 9 19 8   13 8 ,   5

13 14   20 5 12 !   10 5 11   14 5 16

17 6 11 1 21 8   9 3 3   13 14

8 4 8 13 1 8 17   5 4   6 15 8

22 15 8 8 21 .   17 9 3 19 9 6 1 5 4

7 8 3 5 4 20 17   6 5   6 15 8

3 5 11 12 ;   14 5 16 11

7 3 8 17 17 1 4 20   7 8   5 4

14 5 16 11   18 8 5 18 3 8 .

Answer on page 153

Missions Map

Beginning in Capernaum, help each of the disciples pair up, as they did in Episode 2, and find their way to their mission destination. Use the map and clues to figure out who goes where with whom. Write your answers in the table.

PARTNER CLUES
- These two disciples had the same name.
- The tax collector went with the zealot.
- A fisherman was paired with a salesman.
- One of the Sons of Thunder went with the vintner.
- Both of these disciples have six letters in their name.
- The stone mason was matched up with the architect.

LOCATION CLUES
- Andrew had to cross water to get to his destination, but he did not go on the green triangle path.
- One of the Sons of Thunder, whose partner was not Little James, had a mission close to the Mediterranean Sea, but he did not follow the white path.
- The two who journeyed the furthest south were never fisherman.
- Judas travelled north but was not on the yellow path.
- Thaddeus and his partner went across the Sea of Galilee.

Disciple 1	Disciple 2	Path Color	Destination City

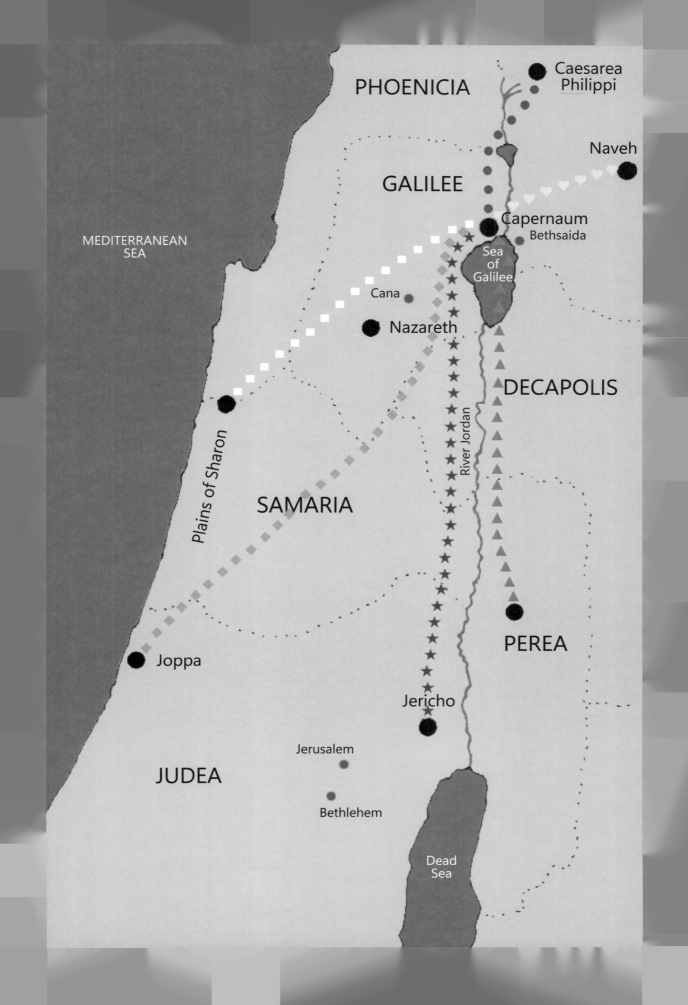

Change the word SICK into WELL one letter at a time.
Use the clues to help you figure out each word.

S I C K

— — — —   touch with tongue

— — — —   hair bugs

— — — —   similar to

— — — —   two-wheel vehicle

— — — —   cook in oven

— — — —   hay bundle

— — — —   round throwing toy

— — — —   ringing instrument

W E L L

Answer on page 154

Alphabet practice!

Practice the next three letters of the Hebrew alphabet!

ZAYIN

ז

This letter sounds like the **z** in Zebedee.

HET

ח

This letter sounds like the **ch** in Bach.

TET

ט

This letter sounds like the **t** in tax.

FULL OF FISH

USE THE LETTERS AND NUMBERS
TO SHOW WHERE EACH OF THESE
PIECES BELONG IN THE PUZZLE.
WE GOT YOU STARTED! ———————→ F8

_____

_____

_____

_____

_____

_____

_____

_____

_____

WORD
IN
WORD

Use the definitions to figure out the words. The letters in the small words will help you figure out the bigger words.

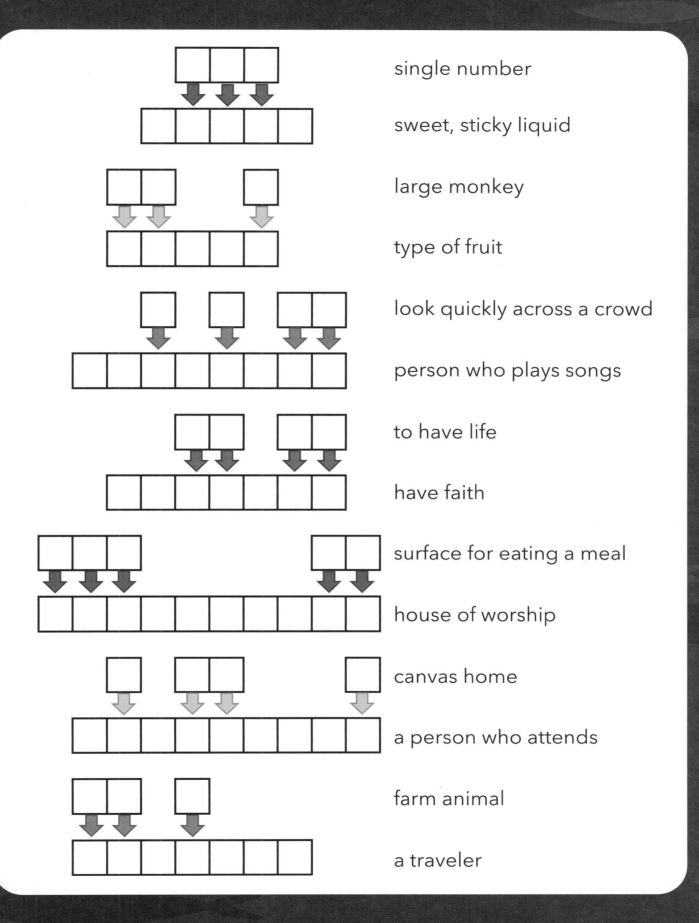

single number

sweet, sticky liquid

large monkey

type of fruit

look quickly across a crowd

person who plays songs

to have life

have faith

surface for eating a meal

house of worship

canvas home

a person who attends

farm animal

a traveler

Answer on page 154

Which Fish?

Each colored fish in the puzzle represents a letter (all five vowels and two consonants). Figure out which fish carries which letter, and then read the prayer Mary and Jesus recited in Episode 3 for the beginning of a new year.

B L 🐟 S S 🐟 🐟 🐟 🐟 Y 🐟 , L 🐟 🐟 🐟

🐟 🐟 G 🐟 , K 🐟 N G 🐟 F T H 🐟

🐟 N V 🐟 🐟 S 🐟 , W H 🐟 H 🐟 S K 🐟 P T

🐟 S 🐟 L 🐟 V 🐟 🐟 N 🐟 S 🐟 S T 🐟 🐟 N 🐟

🐟 S F 🐟 🐟 🐟 N 🐟 T H 🐟 🐟 Y 🐟 🐟 .

W H 🐟 B 🐟 S T 🐟 W S K 🐟 N 🐟 N 🐟 S S ,

🐟 🐟 S T 🐟 🐟 S , 🐟 N 🐟 🐟 🐟 🐟 🐟 M S .

P 🐟 🐟 S 🐟 T Y 🐟 🐟 , 🐟 🐟 N 🐟 🐟

🐟 🐟 🐟 G 🐟 , S 🐟 V 🐟 🐟 🐟 🐟 G N 🐟 V 🐟 🐟

C 🐟 🐟 T 🐟 🐟 N , W H 🐟 H 🐟 S

C H 🐟 S 🐟 N 🐟 S F 🐟 🐟 M 🐟 L L T H 🐟

P 🐟 🐟 P L 🐟 S .

Answer on page 154

Number and Color Code

What did Jesus say about a year of jubilee in Episode 3?

Do the math to find the answers, and then use the number code to figure out which letters go where. The color-coded boxes will help you read what else Jesus said.

A	B	C	D	E	F	G	H	I	J	K	L	M
1	2	3	4	5	6	7	8	9	10	11	12	13

N	O	P	Q	R	S	T	U	V	W	X	Y	Z
14	15	16	17	18	19	20	21	22	23	24	25	26

$\overline{}$ $\overline{}$ $\overline{}$ $\overline{}$ $\overline{}$ $\overline{}$ $\overline{}$ $\overline{}$ $\overline{}$
5x4 4x2 3x3 10+9   4+5 12+7   4x5 2x4 4+1

$\overline{}$ $\overline{}$ $\overline{}$ $\overline{}$ $\overline{}$ $\overline{}$ $\overline{}$ $\overline{}$ $\overline{}$
5x5 3+2 1x1 3x6   5x3 2x3   10x2 4+4 5+0

'

$\overline{}$ $\overline{}$ $\overline{}$ $\overline{}$ $\overline{}$ $\overline{}$ $\overline{}$ $\overline{}$ $\overline{}$ $\overline{}$ '
3x4 12+3 14+4 2x2   10+9   3+3 1x1 11x2 10+5 9x2

$$\overline{1\text{x}1} \qquad \overline{5\text{x}5} \quad \overline{2+3} \quad \overline{1+0} \quad \overline{3\text{x}6} \qquad \overline{5\text{x}3} \quad \overline{4+2}$$

$$\overline{5\text{x}2} \quad \overline{7\text{x}3} \quad \overline{2\text{x}1} \quad \overline{6+3} \quad \overline{6\text{x}2} \quad \overline{2+3} \quad \overline{5\text{x}1} \; , \qquad \overline{1\text{x}1} \quad \overline{2\text{x}7} \quad \overline{3+1}$$

$$\overline{15+5} \quad \overline{5+3} \quad \overline{3+2} \qquad \overline{4\text{x}4} \quad \overline{6+9} \quad \overline{7+8} \quad \overline{3\text{x}6} \; ,$$

$$\overline{2\text{x}1} \quad \overline{6\text{x}3} \quad \overline{11+4} \quad \overline{8+3} \quad \overline{1+4} \quad \overline{7\text{x}2} \quad \overline{6+2} \quad \overline{4+1} \quad \overline{1+0} \quad \overline{9+9} \quad \overline{5\text{x}4} \quad \overline{2+3} \quad \overline{2\text{x}2} \; ,$$

$$\overline{1\text{x}1} \quad \overline{7\text{x}2} \quad \overline{2\text{x}2} \qquad \overline{3\text{x}1} \quad \overline{1\text{x}1} \quad \overline{8+8} \quad \overline{16+4} \quad \overline{5+4} \quad \overline{2\text{x}11} \quad \overline{3+2}$$

$$\overline{1\text{x}1} \quad \overline{9\text{x}2} \quad \overline{5\text{x}1} \qquad \overline{3\text{x}5} \quad \overline{3+3} \quad \overline{2+4} \quad \overline{4+1} \quad \overline{9\text{x}2} \quad \overline{3+2} \quad \overline{2\text{x}2}$$

$$.$$

$$\overline{3\text{x}6} \quad \overline{2+3} \quad \overline{2+2} \quad \overline{4+1} \quad \overline{9+4} \quad \overline{4\text{x}4} \quad \overline{5\text{x}4} \quad \overline{3\text{x}3} \quad \overline{8+7} \quad \overline{2\text{x}7}$$

$$.$$

$$\overline{7+1} \quad \overline{2+3} \quad \overline{13+5} \quad \overline{2+3} \; .$$

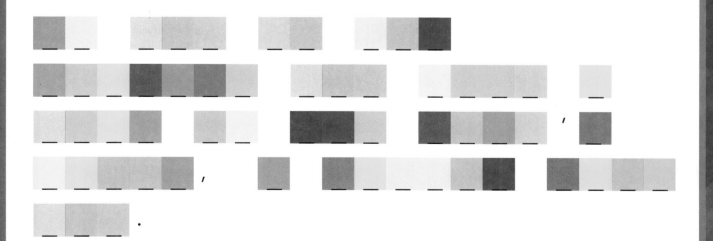

Answer on page 154

Word Search

Find the characters hidden in the word search puzzle.

AARON

AKIVA

ARGO

ASAPH

BATSHEVA

BENJAMIN

DAVID

DION

ELIONAI

FATIYAH

GRAND VIZIER

HANNA

IVO

JEDUTHAN

LEAH

LIVIA

MICHAL

NILI

TELEMACHUS

VERONICA

```
            H B
              A   C
              E   D
      S  C  J      C  L      Q  K
      T  E  L  E  M  A  C  H  U  S  A
   N  T  R  E  I  Z  I  V  D  N  A  R  G
   A  V  E  H  S  T  A  B  B  H  F  S  A
D  H  N  E  B  Y  S  I  E  H  V  A  A  I  A
I  T  O  X  R  A  B  N  A  U  I  T  Y  V  R
O  U  R  V  P  O  J  N  L  A  A  I  D  I  G
N  D  A  H  M  A  N  I  J  K  N  Y  I  L  O
E  A  T  M  A  L  I  R  I  O  A  V  Q
J  D  I  H  I  D  W  C  V  I  H  A  K
N  W  N  M  I  C  H  A  L  F  D
      I  V  O      A  V      E  K
```

WORD CHANGE

L A M E

— — — — opposite of wild

— — — — story

— — — — communicate

W A L K

M U T E

— — — — donkey

— — — — man or boy

— — — — story

T A L K

Change the words LAME into WALK and MUTE into TALK one letter at a time. Use the clues to help you figure out each word.

Practice the next three letters of the Hebrew alphabet!

YOD

This letter sounds like the **y** in you.

י

KAF

This letter sounds like the **k** in key.

כ

LAMED

This letter sounds like the **l** in love.

ל

Which Miracle

On their mission, each group of disciples saw signs and wonders. (Watch Episode 4!) Follow the lines to see which disciples experienced which miracles. Connect the groups with the wonders below.

JOHN & THOMAS

Demon-possessed woman freed

ZEE & MATTHEW

Lame man walks

SIMON & JUDAS

Blind girl sees

BIG JAMES & LITTLE JAMES

Deaf woman hears

PHILIP & ANDREW

Crippled boy healed

THADDEUS & NATHANAEL

Preach the good news

Answer on page 155

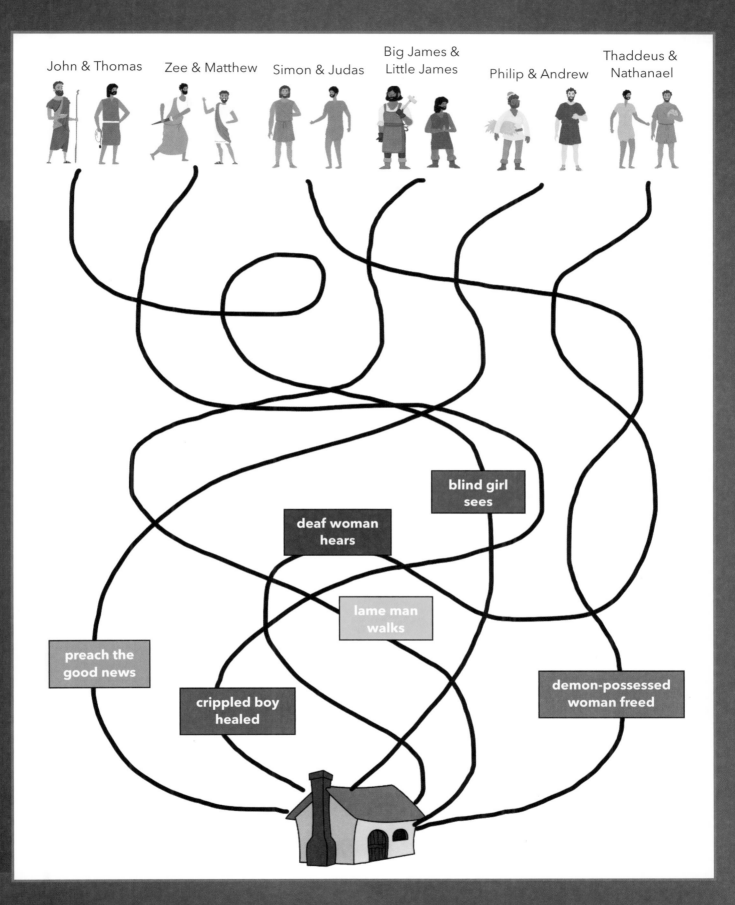

SWORD DRILL

USE THE LETTERS AND NUMBERS
TO SHOW WHERE EACH OF THESE
PIECES BELONG IN THE PUZZLE.
WE GOT YOU STARTED! ⟶ D8

_____

_____

_____

_____

_____

_____

_____

_____

_____

Answer on page 155

75

WORD

IN

WORD

Use the definitions to figure out the words. The letters in the small words will help you figure out the bigger words.

stinging insect

50-year celebration

stick for walking

job Jesus had

herb used in medicine

Jewish house of worship

baby lion

long green vegetable

common Middle Eastern fruit

not eating

walkway

Greek temple for many gods

number after nine

tank to hold water

Answer on page 155

MAZE

When the cistern was broken during Episode Four, it took a long time to get the water needed for drinking and cleaning. Veronica was kind enough to take Eden to a secret spring she had found so they could wash clothes.

Help Veronica and Eden find their way to the spring.

Start
here

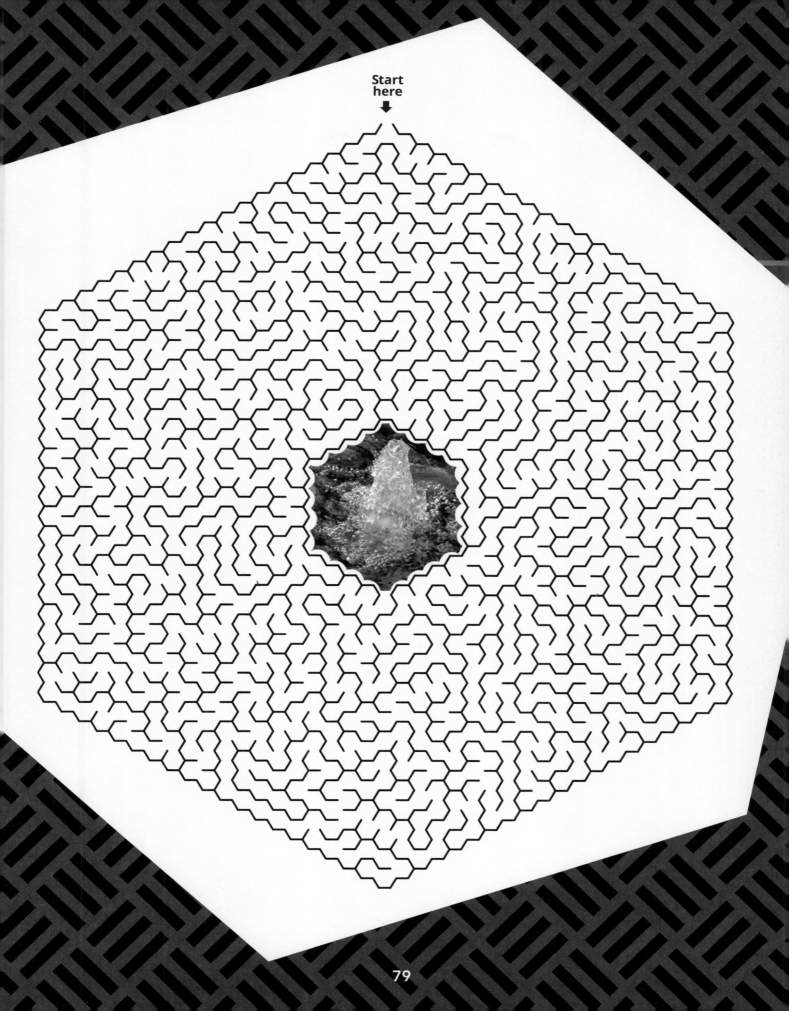

Alphabet practice!

Practice the next three letters of the Hebrew alphabet!

MEM

This letter sounds like the **m** in market.

NUN

This letter sounds like the **n** in net.

SAMEKH

This letter sounds like the **s** in sea.

Picture Puzzle

Use the pictures to read what Jesus said to Veronica in Episode 5 about her miracle.

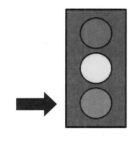   – H + E

_____   _____   _____

4 – F + Y    – G + H

_____   FAITH   _____

 – N + D   YO + **U**

_____   _____   _____.

CROSSWORD FUN

Use the clues to solve the crossword puzzle. Answers with two words are shown in parentheses revealing how many letters are in each word.

ACROSS

2. The name of Jairus' sick daughter
5. The part of Jesus that Veronica touched to be healed
10. One of the disciples in the room when Jairus' daughter was healed (also 6 and 13 Down)
11. What Jesus said healed Veronica
12. The wife of Jairus
14. Jesus called the girl this baby animal when he brought her back to life
15. Where Veronica went to swim after she was healed (3, 2, 7)
17. The disciple Jairus finds at Andrew's house
18. The disciples who found Veronica at the spring (also 4 Down)

DOWN

1. The musical instrument played by the professional mourners
3. What Jesus said Jairus's daughter should do when she got up
4. The disciples who found Veronica at the spring (also 18 Across)
6. One of the disciples in the room when Jairus' daughter was healed (also 13 Down and 10 Across)
7. What Jesus called Veronica after he healed her
8. Jesus said the dead girl was just doing this
9. How many years Veronica suffered
10. What Jesus and the disciples did to clean themselves after the two healings
13. One of the disciples in the room when Jairus' daughter was healed (also 6 Down and 10 Across)
16. The woman who lost a baby while her husband was on a mission

WATCH SEASON 3,
ESPECIALLY
EPISODE 5,
TO HELP YOU
COMPLETE THIS
CROSSWORD!

83

Answer on page 155

MAZE

In Episode 5, Veronica was desperate to get to Jesus so she could be healed, but the crowds were surrounding Him.

Help Veronica get through the crowds so she can touch Jesus.

How many people can you count in this picture? _____

Answer on page 155

WORD FIT

The names of some characters and places are listed here. They only fit into the puzzle one way. Use the number of letters in each word as a clue. We have placed a word to help you get started.

4 LETTERS
ROME

5 LETTERS
AVNER
GAIUS
HEROD
NADAB
NAVEH
PRIMI

6 LETTERS
JAIRUS
JOANNA
YUSSIF

7 LETTERS
ATTICUS
CLAUDIA
DOMINUS
QUINTUS

8 LETTERS
CAIAPHAS
GOVERNOR
NAZARETH
TIBERIUS

9 LETTERS
CAPERNAUM
DECAPOLIS
JERUSALEM

12 LETTERS
JUDEAN DESERT

13 LETTERS
PONTIUS PILATE

Answer on page 155

Alphabet practice!

Practice the next three letters of the Hebrew alphabet!

AYIN

This Hebrew letter is silent.

ע

PE

This letter sounds like the **p** in pot.

פ

TSADI

This letter sounds like the **ts** in eats.

צ

WORD CHANGE

Change the word TENT into CITY one letter at a time.
Use the clues to help you figure out each word.

T E N T

_ _ _ _   a lighter shade

_ _ _ _   breath freshener

_ _ _ _   belongs to me

_ _ _ _   tiny insect

_ _ _ _   quote

C I T Y

Answer on page 156

Picture Search

Find Jesus and His friends hidden in the tent city.

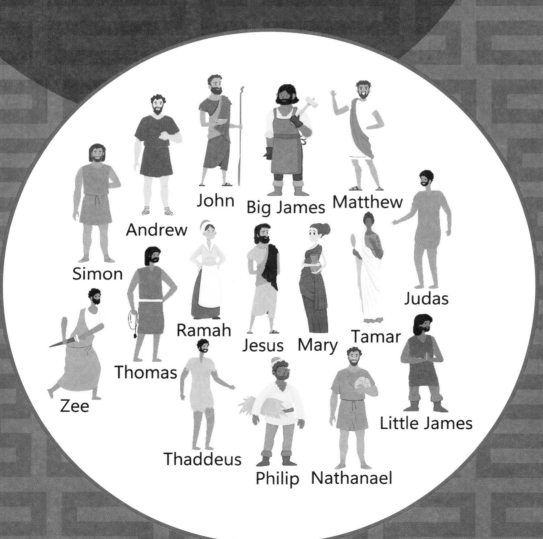

Simon

Andrew

John Big James Matthew

Ramah

Zee Thomas

Jesus Mary Tamar

Judas

Thaddeus

Philip Nathanael

Little James

About Religion

Find the words listed below in the word search puzzle.

ARABIANS
CUSTOMS
FAITH
GENTILES
GREEKS
HELLENISTS
JEWS
LAWS
PHARISEES

PRACTICES
RELIGION
ROMANS
SADDUCEES
SELEUCIDS
TORAH
WORSHIP
ZEALOTS

V G W J F
N E S V Z
P N E X G
I T E W Q
H I C C F
S P C Q R S L U B F G W L S S
J T H C E R E D S W E J E K Z
M K S A E O S D F U B E E O Q
D H D I R W L A W S S E W C Q
E B M L N O L S P I R S G N K
E T D R G
O L A M X
V H L Y D
P R H E Z
K O C S H
S M U Z E
P A S E H
N N T D Z
O S O S E
I S M E A
G E S L L
I C N E O
L I A U T
E T I C S
R C B I X
C A A D T
V R R S D
B P A B C
H T I A F
Q I M B N

A SERIES OF SCROLLS

USE THE LETTERS AND NUMBERS TO SHOW WHERE EACH OF THESE PIECES BELONG IN THE PUZZLE. WE GOT YOU STARTED! ⟶ B1

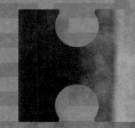

Answer on page 156

WORD IN WORD

Use the definitions to figure out
the words. The letters in the
small words will help you figure
out the bigger words.

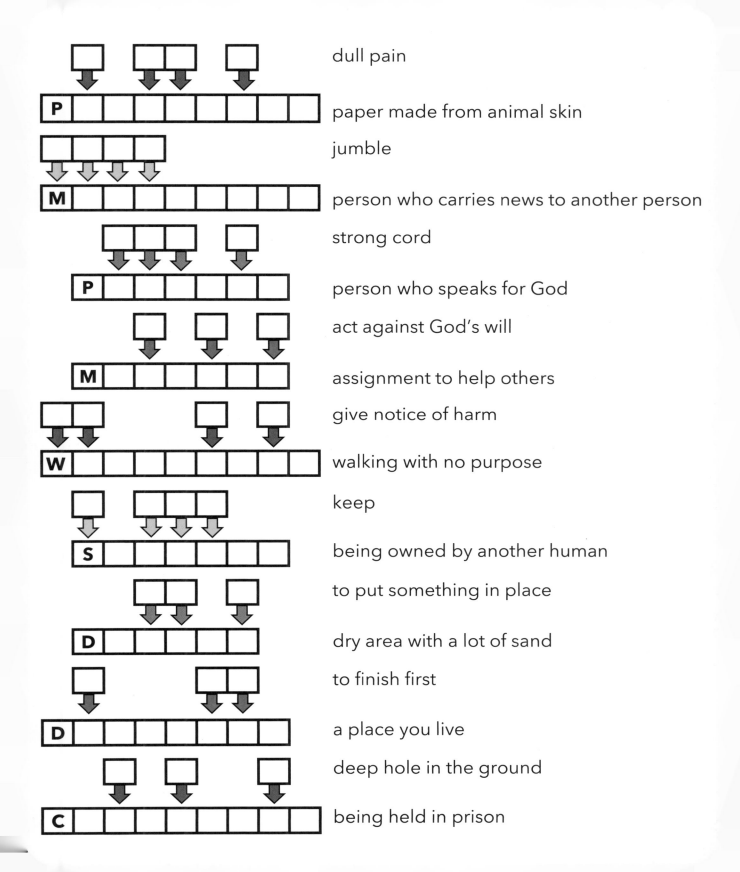

dull pain

paper made from animal skin

jumble

person who carries news to another person

strong cord

person who speaks for God

act against God's will

assignment to help others

give notice of harm

walking with no purpose

keep

being owned by another human

to put something in place

dry area with a lot of sand

to finish first

a place you live

deep hole in the ground

being held in prison

NUMBER CODE

In Episode 6, John the Baptist sent messengers, Avner and Nadab, to Jesus to ask Him a question.

Use the grid to figure out which letters go where, so you can read John's question and the message Jesus told Avner and Nadab to bring back to John. We have given you some numbers to start.

A	B	C	D	E	F	G	H	I	J	K	L	M
			13		1		2				16	

N	O	P	Q	R	S	T	U	V	W	X	Y	Z
	8		23						26		22	

Row 1: 4 5 7 | 6 8 11 | 5 7 4 16 16 6 | 20 2 7

Row 2: 8 14 7 | 21 2 8 | 10 15 | 20 8 | 17 8 3 7 '

Row 3: 8 5 | 15 2 8 11 16 13 | 21 7 | 16 8 8 24 | 1 8 5

?

Row 4: 15 8 3 7 8 14 7 | 7 16 15 7

Row 5: 12 8 | 4 14 13 | 20 7 16 16 | 19 8 2 14 | 21 2 4 20

Row 6: 6 8 11 | 2 7 4 5 | 4 14 13 | 15 7 7 . | 20 2 7

Row 7: 9 16 10 14 13 | 5 7 17 7 10 25 7 | 20 2 7 10 5

Row 8: 15 10 12 2 20 ' | 20 2 7 | 16 4 3 7 | 21 4 16 24 '

Row 9: 20 2 7 | 16 7 18 7 5 15 | 4 5 7

Row 10: 17 16 7 4 14 15 7 13 ' | 20 2 7 | 3 11 20 7

Row 11: 15 18 7 4 24 ' | 20 2 7 | 18 8 8 5 | 2 4 25 7

Row 12: 12 8 8 13 | 14 7 21 15 | 18 5 7 4 17 2 7 13 | 20 8

Row 13: 20 2 7 3 ' | 4 14 13 | 20 2 7 | 13 7 4 13

Row 14: 4 5 7 | 5 4 10 15 7 13 .

99   Answer on page 156

WORD FIT

The names of some historical Israelite weapons are listed here. They only fit into the puzzle one way. Use the number of letters in each word as a clue to where it fits.

3 LETTERS
AXE
BOW

4 LETTERS
CLUB
GOAD
IRON
SICA

5 LETTERS
ARMOR
ARROW
BLADE
KNIFE
RAZOR
SLING
SPEAR
STONE
SWORD

6 LETTERS
DAGGER
HAMMER
HELMET
SHIELD
WEAPON

7 LETTERS
JAVELIN
JAWBONE

9 LETTERS
ARROWHEAD
MILLSTONE

A R M O R

Answer on page 156

Which Fish?

Each colored fish in the puzzle represents a letter (all five vowels and two consonants). Figure out which fish carries which letter, and then read what Jesus said to the religious leaders in Episode 6 about their judgments.

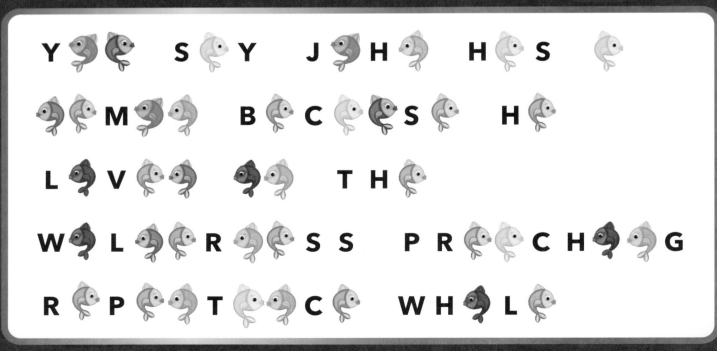

R🐟F🐟S🐟G BR🐟🐟🐟🐟🐟
🐟R🐟🐟K.

🐟🐟W TH🐟 S🐟🐟🐟 F M🐟🐟

C🐟M🐟S PR🐟🐟CH🐟🐟G

S🐟LV🐟T🐟🐟🐟 WH🐟L🐟

🐟🐟T🐟G 🐟🐟🐟 R🐟K🐟G

🐟🐟🐟 🐟🐟🐟 C🐟G, 🐟🐟🐟 🐟'M

C🐟LL🐟🐟 GL🐟TT🐟🐟 🐟🐟🐟

🐟R🐟KR🐟, 🐟 FR🐟🐟🐟

F T🐟X C🐟LL🐟CT🐟RS

🐟🐟🐟 S🐟🐟🐟🐟RS. 🐟T 🐟🐟S

🐟T M🐟TT🐟R WH🐟T 🐟S

P🐟T 🐟🐟 FR🐟🐟T 🐟F Y🐟🐟,

Y🐟🐟 W🐟LL R🐟J🐟CT 🐟T.

LETTER SWAP

Each letter of the alphabet has been paired with another letter, but all the letters got swapped! Use the color code to help you figure out the letter pairs and discover what Jesus said about wisdom in Episode 6.

In the second puzzle, use the color code to read the message.

A	B	C	D	E	F	G	H	I	J	K	L	M
												N

N	O	P	Q	R	S	T	U	V	W	X	Y	Z
M			X							Q		

__ __ ___ ___ ____ __
I T   U E Y   T O O   F R I S   A T

_____ __ _____
R I Z Z O M A M L   S E   S R E T O

_____ ___' __ ___
I H E Y M B   U E Y   I T   U E Y

___ _____ _____
T O O   G A C O T   V R I M L O B

```
__  __  _____  ___
D U   H O Z O M S I M V O   I M B

__  _____  __  ___
T I G C I S A E M   B E   M E S

_____  ___  _____
A L M E H O   S R O   O C A B O M V O

__  ___  _____  __
E W   S R O   J A M L B E N   E W

___!
L E B
```

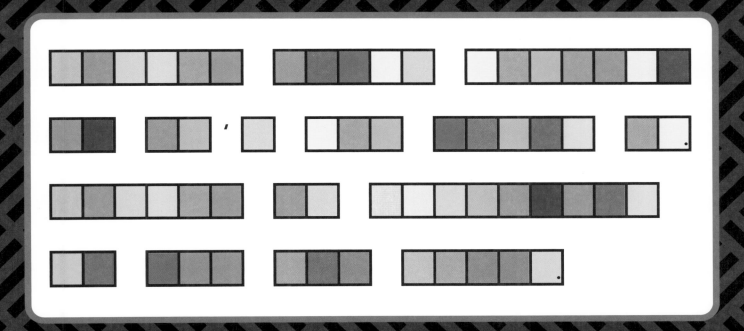

CROSSWORD FUN

Use the clues to solve the crossword.

ACROSS

1. They were out to get Zee
5. Who Thomas hoped to marry
6. John the Baptist's disciples who came looking for Jesus (also 3 Down)
7. True or false: Andrew is a good dancer
10. What Jesus healed on Barnaby's body
11. What Pontius was doing in the tent
15. What the mute man wore around his neck
17. What Jesus gave to Shula
18. What Tamar wouldn't sell for the ministry
19. One word the disciples struggle with
20. What Simon and Gaius fixed together

DOWN

2. One ingredient used on the soil for growing olive trees
3. John the Baptist's disciples who came looking for Jesus (also 6 Across)
4. Where John the Baptist was
8. What Mary was asked to buy a lot of at the market
9. The disciple who went in disguise to the tent city
12. Where Philip and Andrew went
13. Who Atticus was looking for
14. The red spice Eden put on her bread
16. He brought Shula to Jesus for healing

WATCH SEASON 3, ESPECIALLY EPISODE 6, TO HELP YOU COMPLETE THIS CROSSWORD!

Answer on page 157

WORD SCRAMBLE

Unscramble the words below.

HINT: All the words have something to do with the olive oil business.

O E G V R

_ _ _ _ _

E Y R V N I D A

_ _ _ _ _ _ _ _

L I O S

_ _ _ _

L V I O E S

_ _ _ _ _ _

R G P E A S

_ _ _ _ _ _

T E A R W

_ _ _ _ _

G E A V I N R

_ _ _ _ _ _ _

S H A

_ _ _

U S L R U F

_ _ _ _ _ _

E N I P E N L D E S E

_ _ _ _ _ _ _ _ _ _ _

Answer on page 157

Alphabet practice!

Practice the next two letters of the Hebrew alphabet!

QOF

This letter sounds like the **k** in kick.

ק

RESH

This letter sounds like the **r** in rabbi.

ר

LETTER WHEEL

Use the letters in the wheel to complete the prophecy from the prophet Isaiah about the hope for the Gentiles. (See Matthew 12:18.)

B_H_LD, MY S_RV_NT
WH_M _ H_V_ CH_S_N,
MY B_L_V_D W_TH
WH_M MY S__L _S
W_LL PL__S_D.
_ W_LL P_T MY SP_R_T
_P_N H_M, _ND H_
W_LL PR_CL__M J_ST_C_
T_ TH_ G_NT_L_S, _ND
_N H_S N_M_ TH_
G_NT_L_S W_LL H_P_.

Answer on page 157

MARVELOUS MARKET

USE THE LETTERS AND NUMBERS
TO SHOW WHERE EACH OF THESE
PIECES BELONG IN THE PUZZLE.
WE GOT YOU STARTED! ⟶ A8

_____

_____

_____

_____

_____

_____

_____

_____

_____

Answer on page 157

SECRET DECODER

Use the code to decipher what Mary Magdalene said to Matthew in Episode 7 about how difficult their lives had been. Use the numbers to complete the phrase.

Answer on page 158

Word Search

Find the characters hidden in the word search puzzle.

ANTIUS
ARGO
ATTICUS
BARNABY
CAIAPHUS
CANIUS
DION
ELIONAI
FATIYAH
GAIUS
IVO

JAIRUS
JEKEMIAH
LEANDER
LIVIA
MARIUS
MICHAL
NASHON
NILI
SHMUEL
TELEMACHUS
YAELI

```
                        L
                        A
              V    H    R
              E    C    N
         Q    D    I    O    N
         W    L    M    Y    S
       C    I    K    A    A    U    R
       G    H    E    L    R    I    S
O  T  M  I  A  N  O  I  L  E  E  G  A  U  S  H  M  U  E  L  J
J  M  A  A  I  V  I  L  Z  A  O  G  H  G  H  Y  V  P  E
A  J  R  X  S  S  U  I  N  A  C  P  B  A  T  F  Q
   I  Q  I  J  U  M  I  D  D  J  A  U  Y  W  F
      R  S  U  E  H  N  E  D  R  I  A  I  G
      U  N  S  K  C  R  N  Y  A  L  T
      I  S  X  Q  E  A  U  T  C  U  A
   W  T  D  F  A  B  M  M  N  I  H  F  F
   H  N  U  T  Y  F     I  E  A  S  V  B
   Y  T  A  T  M  S        A  L  S  R  R  I
      P  N  I  V  O           H  E  H  A  Z
   I  O  C  L                    T  O  I  M
   A  U                          N     D
   S                                   K
```

CROSSWORD FUN

Use the clues to solve the crossword. Answers with two words are shown in parentheses revealing how many letters are in each word.

ACROSS

3. The disciple who hurt his foot

5. What the old man Elionai really wanted to share with Matthew

7. Where Andrew & Philip created a crisis with their preaching

9. What Matthew had hidden in a box (6, 7)

11. The fourteenth day of this month was for gladness and feasting

12. The parable about this event upset many people in the Decapolis

14. The kind of professional Marius thought Simon was

15. Who Jesus asked to stay behind and wait for Simon

DOWN

1. The number of knots and threads used to make prayer tassels

2. The disciple who smashed a crate on his roof

4. He took Simon into his house for questioning

6. There are 613 of these in the law

8. Jairus read the Bible story of this woman to his daughter Nili

10. The disciple who rearranged Andrew's cabinet

13. The deaf and mute man who Jesus healed

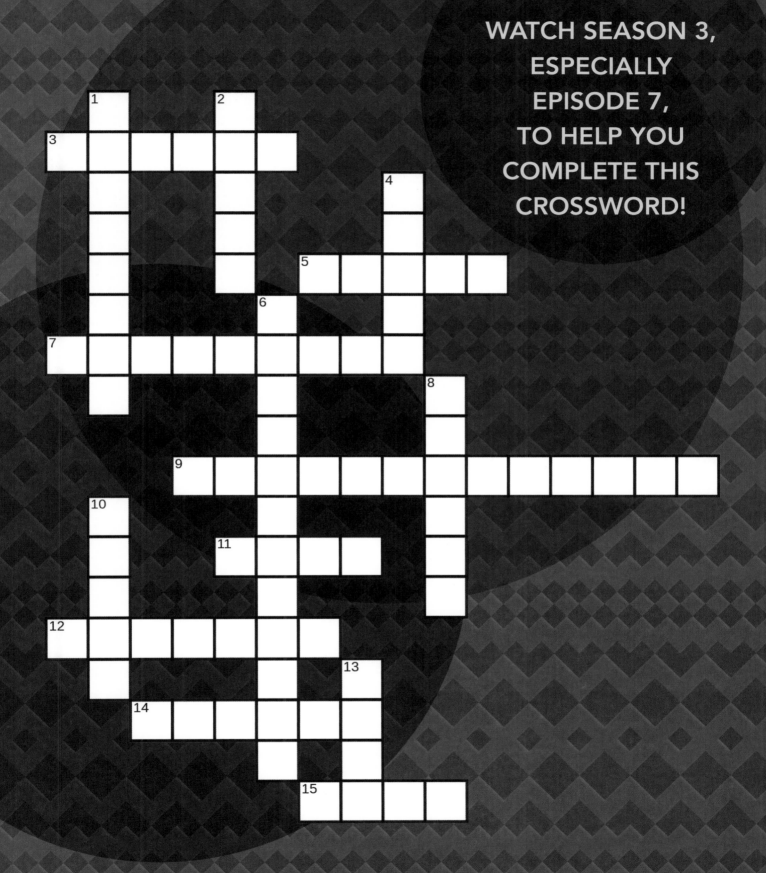

WATCH SEASON 3, ESPECIALLY EPISODE 7, TO HELP YOU COMPLETE THIS CROSSWORD!

Answer on page 158

LETTER DROP

Use the definitions to figure out the words. The letters with arrows "drop" down into the boxes below them to help you complete each word.

(Extra clue: colored arrows represent the same letter throughout)

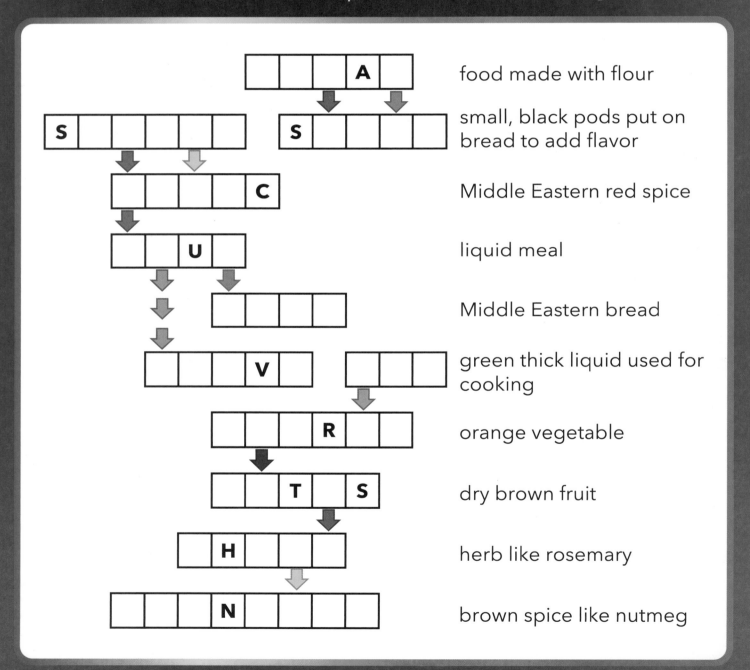

food made with flour

small, black pods put on bread to add flavor

Middle Eastern red spice

liquid meal

Middle Eastern bread

green thick liquid used for cooking

orange vegetable

dry brown fruit

herb like rosemary

brown spice like nutmeg

Alphabet practice!

Practice the last two letters of the Hebrew alphabet!

SHIN

This letter sounds like the **sh** in ship.

TAW

This letter sounds like the **t** in teach.

Which Fish?

Each colored fish in the puzzle represents a letter (all five vowels and two consonants). Figure out which fish carries which letter, and then read the psalm that Asaph presented to King David.

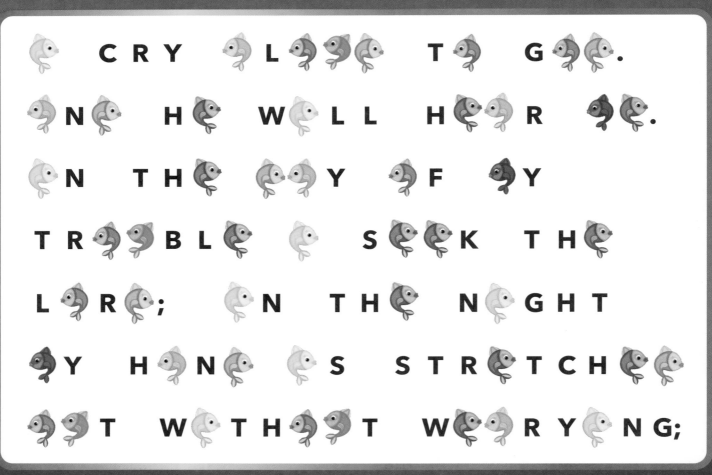

I CRY ALOUD TO GOD.

AND HE WILL HEAR ME.

IN THE DAY OF MY

TROUBLE I SEEK THE

LORD; IN THE NIGHT

MY HAND IS STRETCHED

OUT WITHOUT WEARYING;

🐟Y S🐟🐟L R🐟F🐟S🐟S T🐟
B🐟 C🐟🐟F🐟RT🐟🐟. WH🐟N 🐟
R🐟🐟🐟🐟B🐟R G🐟🐟, 🐟 🐟🐟🐟N;
WH🐟N 🐟 🐟🐟🐟🐟T🐟T🐟, 🐟Y
SP🐟R🐟T F🐟🐟NTS. Y🐟🐟
H🐟L🐟 🐟Y 🐟Y🐟L🐟🐟S 🐟P🐟N;
🐟 🐟🐟 S🐟 TR🐟🐟BL🐟🐟
TH🐟T 🐟 C🐟NN🐟T SP🐟🐟K.
🐟 C🐟NS🐟🐟🐟R TH🐟 🐟🐟YS
🐟F 🐟L🐟, TH🐟 Y🐟🐟RS
L🐟NG 🐟G🐟. 🐟 S🐟🐟, "L🐟T
🐟🐟 R🐟🐟🐟🐟B🐟R 🐟Y S🐟NG
🐟N TH🐟 N🐟GHT; L🐟T 🐟🐟
🐟🐟🐟🐟T🐟T🐟 🐟N 🐟Y H🐟🐟RT."

BOUNTIFUL BOWLS

USE THE LETTERS AND NUMBERS TO SHOW WHERE EACH OF THESE PIECES BELONG IN THE PUZZLE. WE GOT YOU STARTED! ⟶ <u>D8</u>

_____

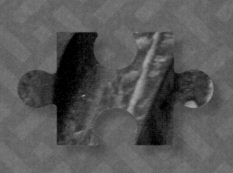

_____

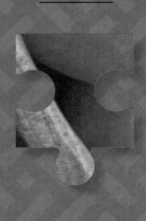

_____

_____

_____

_____

_____

_____

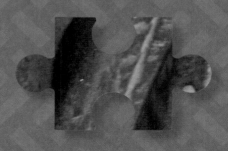

_____

Answer on page 158

LETTER SWAP

Each letter of the alphabet has been paired with another letter, but all the letters got swapped! Figure out the letter pairs and discover what Jesus said to His disciples about the size of their faith. (See Luke 17:6.)

A	B	C	D	E	F	G	H	I	J	K	L	M
I							M	A		X		H

N	O	P	Q	R	S	T	U	V	W	X	Y	Z
		V	S	R			Q		K			

```
—  — —    —  — —    — — —    — — — — —
A  C      U  E  Y    M  I  L    C  I  A  B  M

—  — —    — — — —    — —    —    — — — — —
B  M  O    R  A  J  O    E  C    I    P  S  I  A  W

—  —    — — — — — —    — — — —'
E  C    H  Y  R  B  I  S  L    R  O  O  L

— — —    — — — — —    — — —    — —    —"
U  E  Y    F  E  Y  D  L    R  I  U    B  E    I

— — — — — — —    — — — — ',    — —
H  Y  D  T  O  S  S  U    B  S  O  O     T  O

— — — — — — —    — — —
Y  G  S  E  E  B  O  L    I  W  L

— — — — — —    — —    — — —
G  D  I  W  B  O  L    A  W    B  M  O

— — — '"    — — —    — —    — — — — —
R  O  I     I  W  L    A  B    N  E  Y  D  L

— — — —    — — — — .
E  T  O  U    U  E  Y
```

PICTURE PUZZLE

Use the pictures to help you figure out what Jesus said to His disciples about faith. (See Matthew 17:20.)

 – G – T   YO + **U**    – I + A    – CE + ITH

_____   _____   _____

 – B + L   G +

_____ A _____ OF _____

   YO + **U**    – H + S   **2** – W

_____ , _____ COULD _____   _____

   – L + M    – G + M

A _____   "_____   _____

   2 – W   &   person sitting – S

_____   _____ THERE,"   _____   _____

 – H + W   heart – L + M   &   **0**

_____   _____ , _____   _____

 – H + W   bee – E   **4** – U   YO + **U**

_____   _____ IMPOSSIBLE _____   _____ .

NUMBER CODE

Jesus said these words to Philip about faith in Episode 8.

Use the grid to figure out which letters belong to which numbers. We have given you some numbers to start.

A	B	C	D	E	F	G	H	I	J	K	L	M
3						21	6		23	16		

N	O	P	Q	R	S	T	U	V	W	X	Y	Z
18	5		14			4		17		26		

$$\overline{10}\ \overline{4}\ '\ \overline{7}\quad \overline{18}\ \overline{5}\ \overline{4}\quad \overline{3}\ \overline{15}\ \overline{5}\ \overline{22}\ \overline{4}\quad \overline{7}\ \overline{10}\ \overline{24}\ \overline{2}\ \cdot$$

$$\overline{10}\ \overline{4}\ '\ \overline{7}\quad \overline{3}\ \overline{15}\ \overline{5}\ \overline{22}\ \overline{4}\quad \overline{20}\ \overline{6}\ \overline{5}\quad \overline{25}\ \overline{5}\ \overline{22}\ \overline{12}$$

$$\overline{13}\ \overline{3}\ \overline{10}\ \overline{4}\ \overline{6}\quad \overline{10}\ \overline{7}\quad \overline{10}\ \overline{18}\ \cdot\quad \overline{10}\ \overline{13}\quad \overline{25}\ \overline{5}\ \overline{22}$$

$$\overline{3}\ \overline{12}\ \overline{2}\quad \overline{7}\ \overline{2}\ \overline{9}\ \overline{22}\ \overline{12}\ \overline{2}\quad \overline{10}\ \overline{18}\quad \overline{25}\ \overline{5}\ \overline{22}\ \overline{12}$$

$$\overline{13}\ \overline{3}\ \overline{10}\ \overline{4}\ \overline{6}\quad \overline{10}\ \overline{18}\quad \overline{21}\ \overline{5}\ \overline{19}\ '\quad \overline{4}\ \overline{12}\ \overline{22}\ \overline{7}\ \overline{4}\ \overline{10}\ \overline{18}\ \overline{21}$$

$$\overline{10}\ \overline{18}\quad \overline{6}\ \overline{10}\ \overline{7}\quad \overline{11}\ \overline{12}\ \overline{5}\ \overline{8}\ \overline{10}\ \overline{7}\ \overline{2}\ \overline{7}\ '$$

$$\overline{9}\ \overline{6}\ \overline{5}\ \overline{5}\ \overline{7}\ \overline{10}\ \overline{18}\ \overline{21}\quad \overline{6}\ \overline{10}\ \overline{7}\quad \overline{20}\ \overline{10}\ \overline{1}\ \overline{1}\quad \overline{13}\ \overline{5}\ \overline{12}$$

$$\overline{25}\ \overline{5}\ \overline{22}\ \overline{12}\quad \overline{1}\ \overline{10}\ \overline{13}\ \overline{2}\quad \overline{10}\ \overline{18}\ \overline{7}\ \overline{4}\ \overline{2}\ \overline{3}\ \overline{19}\quad \overline{5}\ \overline{13}$$

$$\overline{25}\ \overline{5}\ \overline{22}\ \overline{12}\quad \overline{5}\ \overline{20}\ \overline{18}\ '\quad \overline{4}\ \overline{10}\ \overline{18}\ \overline{25}\quad \overline{7}\ \overline{10}\ \overline{24}\ \overline{2}\ \overline{19}$$

$$\overline{13}\ \overline{3}\ \overline{10}\ \overline{4}\ \overline{6}\quad \overline{10}\ \overline{7}\quad \overline{2}\ \overline{18}\ \overline{5}\ \overline{22}\ \overline{21}\ \overline{6}\ \cdot$$

WORD CHANGE

Change the word SEED into HOPE and then
HOPE into HEAL one letter at time.
Use the clues to help you figure out each word.

S E E D

_ _ _ _ pay attention

_ _ _ _ grabbed onto

_ _ _ _ to carry

_ _ _ _ open space

H O P E

HOPE

_ _ _ _   tube for water

_ _ _ _   have people over

_ _ _ _   put up a message

_ _ _ _   annoying animal

_ _ _ _   highest quality

_ _ _ _   win

_ _ _ _   to make warm

HEAL

Answer on page 159

WORD IN WORD

Use the definitions to figure out the small words. The letters in the small words will help you figure out the bigger words. Choose your answers from the list below.

ANDREW

BIG JAMES

JOHN

JUDAS

LITTLE JAMES

MARY

MATTHEW

NATHANAEL

PHILIP

RAMAH

SIMON

TAMAR

THADDEUS

THOMAS

ZEE

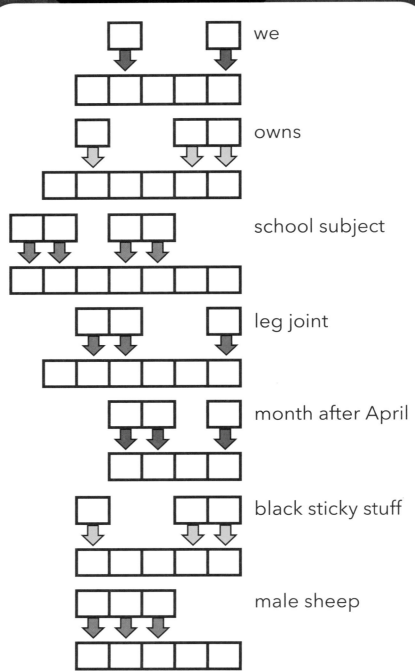

we

owns

school subject

leg joint

month after April

black sticky stuff

male sheep

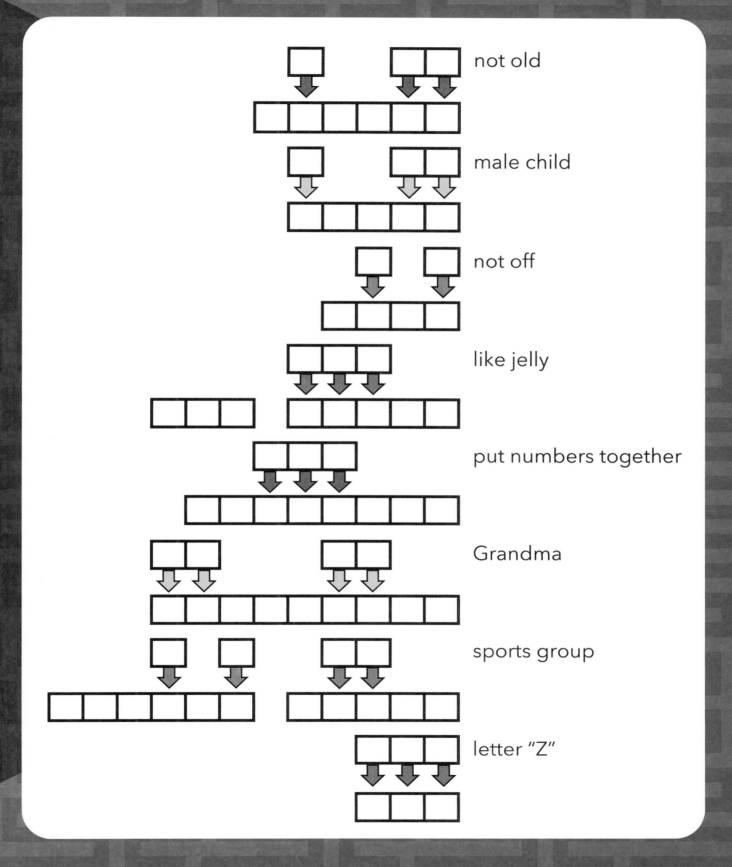

not old

male child

not off

like jelly

put numbers together

Grandma

sports group

letter "Z"

Answer on page 159

SECRET DECODER

Use the code to decipher the parable Jesus told about two sons working for their father in Matthew 21. Use the numbers to complete the second puzzle that asks a question. Then answer the question with your own thoughts.

※	♦	●	✦	⌘	🐟	◈	◗	⏶	✝	◉	🕯	⚡
A	B	C	D	E	F	G	H	I	J	K	L	M

⚷	♪	□	✕	💰	✻	☁	⚙	★	☼	✿	✡	❖
N	O	P	Q	R	S	T	U	V	W	X	Y	Z

1

※ ⚡ ※ ⚷   ◗ ※ ✦   ☁ ☼ ♪   ✻ ♪ ⚷ ✻ .

2

◗ ⌘   ☼ ⌘ ⚷   ☁   ☁ ♪   ☁ ◗ ⌘

3

🐟 ⏶ 💰 ✻ ☁   ※ ⚷ ✦   ✻ ※ ⏶ ✦ '

   " ✻ ♪ ⚷ '   ◈ ♪   ※ ⚷ ✦   ☼ ♪ 💰 ◉

9

⏶ ⚷   ☁ ◗ ⌘   ★ ⏶ ⚷ ⌘ ✡ ※ 💰 ✦

   " .

☁ ♪ ✦ ※ ✡   ※ ⚷ ✦   ◗ ⌘

   " '

※ ⚷ ✻ ☼ ⌘ 💰 ⌘ ✦   ⏶   ☼ ⏶ 🕯 🕯

Answer on page 160

MAZE

Jesus fed 5,000 people with only five loaves and two fish! Help the disciples get through the maze to get back to Jesus. Collect the baskets of leftover food on the way.

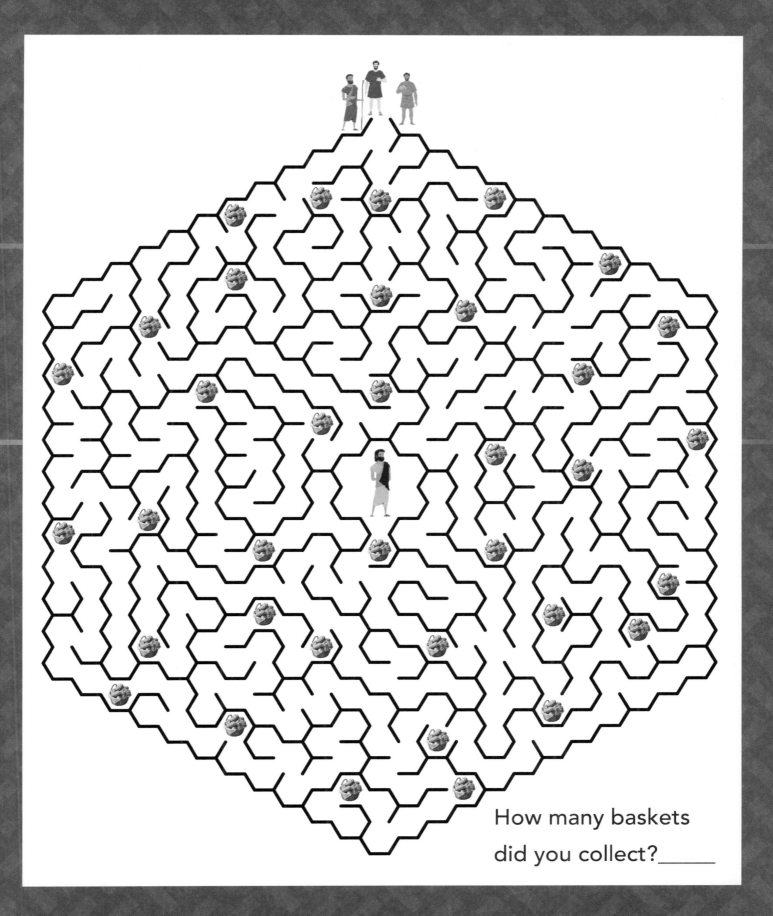

How many baskets
did you collect?_____

Answer on page 160

Word Search

Find the highlighted words in the word search puzzle. Jesus prayed this to His Father in Matthew 11:25.

THANK YOU, FATHER, LORD of HEAVEN and EARTH, that you HAVE HIDDEN THESE THINGS FROM the WISE and UNDERSTANDING and REVEALED THEM to LITTLE CHILDREN.

```
          K   F   R   Y   F
      W   I   S   E   O   T   Y   N   N
    A   O   Q   V   U   V   Q   R   E   E   B
    F   W   K   E       K   M   M       D   V   D   G
    X   X   A   E       E   O   E       D   A   R   T
  M   N   L   R   E     F   R   H       I   E   O   K   Y
  F   E   L   U   C     K   F   T       H   H   L   S   S
  D   U   N   D   E   R   S   T   A   N   D   I   N   G   D
  C   H   I   L   D   R   E   N   U   S   G   N   I   H   T
  Z   F   X       L   I   T   T   L   E   D       X   L   D
  K   A   T       E   S   E   H   T       Q   O   F
  W   M   T   P                       E   V   A   H
      X   O   H   T   H   A   N   K   W   D   N
          I   V   E   Z   H   T   R   A   E
              Y   R   E   U   Q
```

141

PARABLE OF THE SOWER

Jesus told the crowds a story, or *parable*, about a sower who was planting seeds. As he threw the seeds in different places, certain things happened to the seeds.

Complete the sentences below with the picture letters that tell the correct story. Extra clue: follow the lines on the next page to help you figure it out.

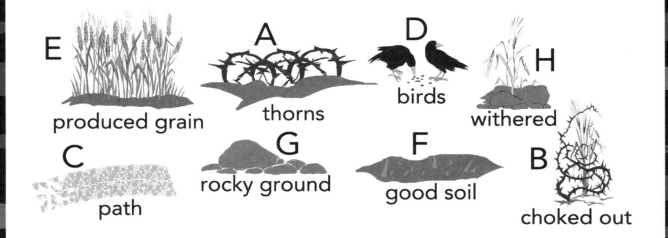

E produced grain
A thorns
D birds
H withered
C path
G rocky ground
F good soil
B choked out

1. Some seeds fell along the _____ and the _____ came and ate them.

2. Other seeds fell on the _____ where there was not much soil. They sprang up quickly, but when the sun rose, they _____ because their roots did not go deep.

3. Some seeds fell among the _____ , and as they grew, they were _____ .

4. Other seeds fell on _____ and they _____ .

Answer on page 160

YOU CAN FIND THIS PARABLE IN MATTHEW 13, MARK 4, AND LUKE 8.

WORDS FROM WORDS

M O
Y T
S R

Use the letters in the circle to create words in the boxes. There is one word that uses all of the letters.

_ _ _ _ _ _ _

S _ _ _ _   S _ _ _ _

M _ _ _   R _ _ _   R _ _ _

S _ _ _   T _ _ _

R _ _   S _ _   S _ _   T _ _   T _ _

M _   O _   S _   T _

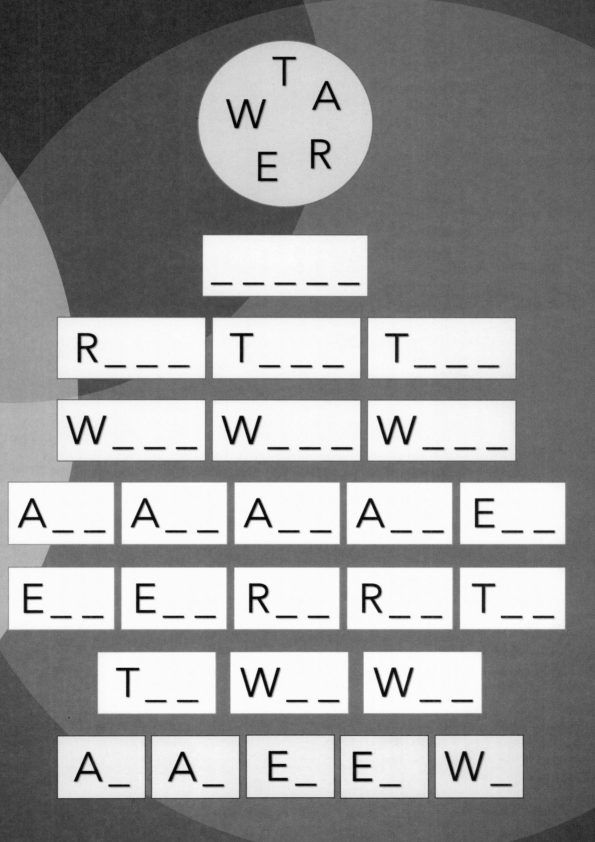

Answer on page 160

LETTER WHEEL

Use the letters in the wheel to read the words Jesus spoke about resting in Him. (See Matthew 11:28-30.) Letters can be used multiple times.

"C_M_ T_ M_ _LL WH_ L_B_R _ND _R_ H__VY L_D_N, _ND, _ W_LL G_V_ Y__ R_ST. T_K_ MY Y_K_ _P_N Y__, _ND L__RN FR_M M_, F_R _ _M G_NTL_ _ND L_WLY _N H__RT, _ND Y__ W_LL F_ND R_ST F_R Y__R S__LS. F_R MY Y_K_ _S __SY _ND MY B_RD_N _S L_GHT!"

Answer on page 160

WORDS from FISH

Collect the letters from the fish and then unscramble them so you can hear what Simon cried out in Episode 8 when Jesus saved him from drowning. Each letter can only be used once.

_ _ _ _ ' _ _ _ _ _ _ _ _ _ _!

ANSWER KEY

PAGE 4

A4	B2	F5
F8	E7	E4
A6	C5	D3

PAGE 7

Therefore I tell you, do not be anxious about your life, what you will eat or what you will drink, nor about your body, what you will put on. Which of you by being anxious…

can add a single hour to his span of life.

PAGES 8-9

A	B	C	D	E	F	G	H	I	J	K	L	M
9	18	4	25	12	2	14	26	3	6	16	10	21

N	O	P	Q	R	S	T	U	V	W	X	Y	Z
11	22	1	17	5	20	8	13	24	7	15	19	23

"Judge not that you not be judged. For with the judgment you pronounce you will be judged, and with the measure you use it will be measured to you."

PAGES 12-13

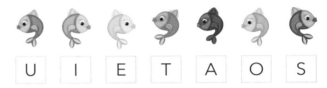

U	I	E	T	A	O	S

"The Gentiles seek after all these things, and your heavenly Father knows that you need them all. But seek first the kingdom of God and His righteousness, and all these things will be added to you."

PAGE 15

PAGES 16-17

"Whatever you wish that others would do to you do also to them, for this is the Law and the Prophets."

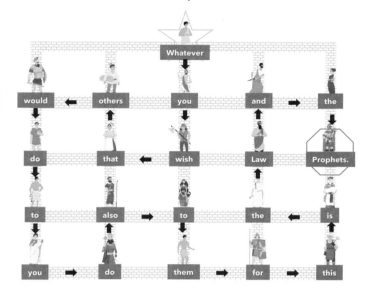

PAGE 19

"Is not LIFE more than FOOD, and the BODY more than CLOTHING? Look at the BIRDS of the AIR: they neither SOW nor REAP nor gather into BARNS, and yet your HEAVENLY Father FEEDS them. Are you not of more VALUE than they?"

PAGES 20-21

"Our Father in heaven, hallowed be your name. Your kingdom come, your will be done, on earth as it is in heaven. Give us this day our daily bread, and forgive us our debts, as we also have forgiven our debtors. And lead us not into temptation, but deliver us from evil."

PAGE 23

"Do not lay up for yourselves treasures on earth where moth and rust destroy and where thieves break in and steal. Lay up for yourselves treasures in heaven, where neither moth nor rust destroys and where thieves do not break in and steal. For where your treasure is, there your heart will be also."

PAGE 25

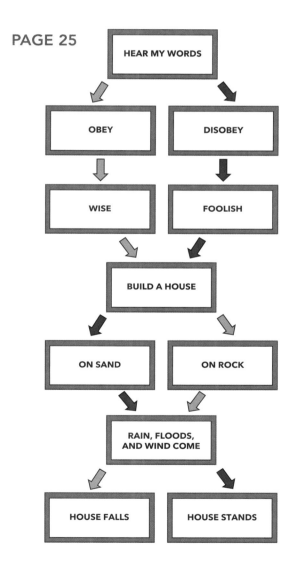

PAGES 26-27

O	N	A	E	H	U	I

"The Lord bless you and keep you. May the Lord make His face shine on you and be gracious to you. The Lord turn His face to you and give you peace."

PAGE 30

C2	A3	D7
F8	A7	D4
C5	E1	F2

PAGE 35

Across: 2. Eden 5. Jairus
9. Alphaeus 10. Matthew
11. Mary Magdalene

Down: 1. Judas 3. Thomas
4. Big James 5. Joanna
6. Veronica 7. Nathanael
8. Zebedee 12. Yussif
13. Andrew

PAGES 36-37

"You are my leaders. For the mission I have for you, it's best that you spread out and not be concentrated in one place. The kingdom of heaven is at hand. While you are on this mission, you will heal the sick and lame by anointing them with oil; you will cast out demons. While you're on this mission, I grant you this authority. Someday you will have it all the time.

I don't need you to feel anything to do great things."

PAGE 39

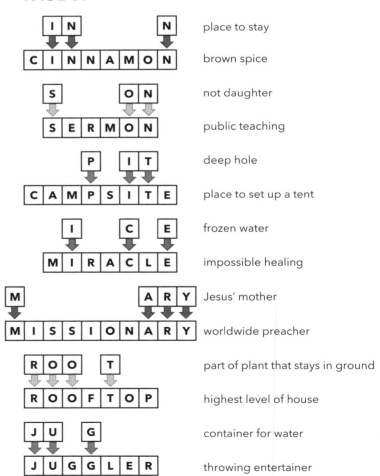

place to stay
brown spice
not daughter
public teaching
deep hole
place to set up a tent
frozen water
impossible healing
Jesus' mother
worldwide preacher
part of plant that stays in ground
highest level of house
container for water
throwing entertainer

PAGE 40

11 fires

PAGES 42-43

A	B	C	D	E	F	G	H	I	J	K	L	M
16	3	17	11	7	20	10	22	2	26	15	19	5

N	O	P	Q	R	S	T	U	V	W	X	Y	Z
12	6	4	24	1	21	8	13	9	14	23	18	25

"You received without paying; now give without pay. Whatever town or village you enter, find out who is worthy in it and stay there until you depart. If anyone will not receive you or listen to your words, shake off the dust from your feet when you leave that house or town. Don't waste your time."

PAGES 44-45

To know how to still praise God in spite of this, to know how to focus on all that matters so much more than the body. To show people how you can be patient with your suffering here on earth because you know you'll spend eternity with no suffering. Not everyone can understand that. Hold on a little longer, and when you find true strength because of your weakness, and when you do great things in my name in spite of this, the impact will last for generations. You will be healed… it's only a matter of time.

PAGE 49

Across: 1. Joseph 3. Raisins 5. Key
6. Zebedee 7. Philip 9. Little James
12. Gaius 14. Martha 15. Bridle 17. Judas

Down: 2. Olive oil 4. Zee 5. Knife 8. Mint
10. Lazarus 11. Andrew 13. Simon 16. Dog

PAGES 50-51

Mary's house – Red – Mary, Tamar, Ramah

Zebedee's house – Green – Big James, John, Thomas

Simon & Eden's house – Blue – Simon, Nathanael, Zee

Andrew's house – Yellow – Andrew, Philip

PAGES 52-55

A	B	C	D	E	F	G	H	I	J	K	L	M
9	7	22	12	8	10	20	15	1	--	21	3	13

N	O	P	Q	R	S	T	U	V	W	X	Y	Z
4	5	18	--	11	17	6	16	19	2	--	14	--

O Lord, how many are my foes! Many are rising against me; many are saying of my soul, "There is no salvation for him in God." But you, O Lord, are a shield about me, my glory, and the lifter of my head. I cried aloud to the Lord, and he answered me from his holy hill. I lay down and slept; I woke again, for the Lord sustained me.

I will not be afraid of many thousands of people who have set themselves against me all around. Arise, O Lord! Save me, O my God! For you strike all my enemies on the cheek. Salvation belongs to the Lord; your blessing be on your people. —Psalm 3 ESV

PAGE 56

Big James & Little James – white square – Plains of Sharon
Matthew & Zee – purple star – Jericho
Simon & Judas – blue circle – Caesarea Philippa
John & Thomas – orange diamond – Joppa

PAGE 58

SICK, LICK, LICE, LIKE, BIKE,
BAKE, BALE, BALL, BELL, WELL

PAGE 60

B1   D4   D2

E3   B5   D7

F5   A3   B6

PAGE 63

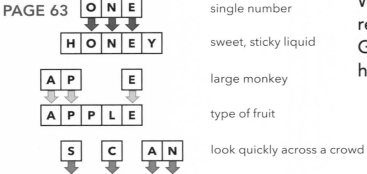

O N E	single number
H O N E Y	sweet, sticky liquid
A P E	large monkey
A P P L E	type of fruit
S C A N	look quickly across a crowd
M U S I C I A N	person who plays songs
L I V E	to have life
B E L I E V E	have faith
T A B L E	surface for eating a meal
T A B E R N A C L E	house of worship
T E N T	canvas home
A T T E N D A N T	a person who attends
P I G	farm animal
P I L G R I M	a traveler

PAGES 64-65

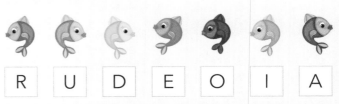

R	U	D	E	O	I	A

"Blessed are you, Lord our God, King of the universe, who has kept us alive and sustained us for another year. Who bestows kindness, restores, and redeems. Praise to you, Adonai our God, sovereign over creation, who has chosen us from all the peoples."

PAGES 66-67

This is the year of the Lord's favor, a year of jubilee, and the poor, brokenhearted, and captive are offered redemption. Here.

If you do not realize you need a year of the Lord's favor, I cannot save you.

PAGE 70

LAME, TAME, TALE, TALK, WALK

MUTE, MULE, MALE, TALE, TALK

PAGE 72

JOHN & THOMAS — Blind girl sees
ZEE & MATTHEW — Crippled boy healed
SIMON & JUDAS — Lame man walks
BIG JAMES & LITTLE JAMES — Preach the good news
PHILIP & ANDREW — Demon-possessed woman freed
THADDEUS & NATHANAEL — Deaf woman hears

PAGE 74

A7	A4	B6
B2	F6	C4
E5	D1	E3

PAGE 77

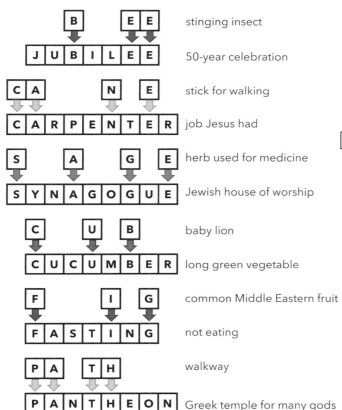

Clue	Answer
stinging insect	BEE
50-year celebration	JUBILEE
stick for walking	CANE
job Jesus had	CARPENTER
herb used for medicine	SAGE
Jewish house of worship	SYNAGOGUE
baby lion	CUB
long green vegetable	CUCUMBER
common Middle Eastern fruit	FIG
not eating	FASTING
walkway	PATH
Greek temple for many gods	PANTHEON
number after nine	TEN
tank to hold water	CISTERN

PAGE 81

"Go in peace. Your faith has made you well."

PAGE 83

Across: 2. Nili 5. Garment 10. Simon 11. Faith 12. Michal 14. Lamb 16. Sea of Galilee 17. Judas 18. Zee

Down: 1. Flute 4. Nathanael 6. John 7. Daughter 8. Sleeping 9. Twelve 10. Swim 13. Big James 16. Eden

PAGE 84

534 people

PAGE 87

PAGE 89

TENT, TINT, MINT, MINE, MITE, CITE, CITY

PAGE 94

F7	D7	C4
C6	F3	D2
A3	B8	E5

PAGE 97

PAGES 98-99

A	B	C	D	E	F	G	H	I	J	K	L	M
4	9	17	13	7	1	12	2	10	19	24	16	3

N	O	P	Q	R	S	T	U	V	W	X	Y	Z
14	8	18	23	5	15	20	11	25	21	26	6	22

"Are you really the one who is to come, or should we look for someone else?"
"Go and tell John what you hear and see. The blind receive their sight, the lame walk, the lepers are cleansed, the mute speak, the poor have good new preached to them, and the dead are raised."

PAGE 101

PAGES 102-103

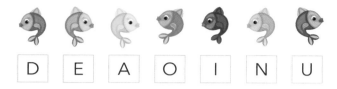

| D | E | A | O | I | N | U |

"You say John has a demon because he lived in the wilderness preaching repentance while refusing bread and drink. Now the Son of Man comes preaching salvation while eating and drinking and dancing, and I'm called a glutton and drunkard, a friend of tax collectors and sinners. It does not matter what is put in front of you, you will reject it."

PAGES 104-105

A	B	C	D	E	F	G	H	I	J	K	L	M
I	D	V	B	O	W	L	R	A	K	J	G	N
N	O	P	Q	R	S	T	U	V	W	X	Y	Z
M	E	Z	X		T	S	Y	C	F	Q	U	P

"As you see what is happening to those around you, as you see lives changed by repentance and salvation, do not ignore the evidence of the kingdom of God!

Wisdom means nothing if it's not acted on. Wisdom is justified by all her works."

PAGE 107

Across: 1. Zealots 5. Ramah 6. Avner 7. False 10. Leg 11. Reading 15. Chalkboard 17. Sight 18. Necklace 19. Soon 20. Cistern

Down: 2. Ash 3. Nadab 4. Prison 8. Sulfur 9. Zee 12. Decapolis 13. Pontius 14. Sumac 16. Barnaby

PAGE 108

GROVE, VINEYARD, SOIL, OLIVES, GRAPES, WATER, VINEGAR, ASH, SULFUR, PINE NEEDLES

PAGE 111

Behold, My servant whom I have chosen. My beloved with whom My soul is well pleased. I will put My Spirit upon him, and he will proclaim justice to the Gentiles, and in his name the Gentiles will hope.

PAGE 112

E5	E7	E1
D8	C6	B2
F3	A4	D4

PAGES 114-115

We think like is full of scarcity and not abundance. But then there are those times when, out of nowhere, the whole world somehow expresses its longing to be whole. And suddenly God steps in. And we're pulled out of our blindness, and we're invited to redemption. I know I was. I know you were.

PAGE 119

Across: 3. Philip 5. Faith 7. Decapolis 9. Prayer tassels 11. Adar 12. Banquet 14. Doctor 15. John

Down: 1. Thirteen 2. Simon 4. Gaius 6. Commandments 8. Esther 10. Judas 13. Argo

PAGE 120

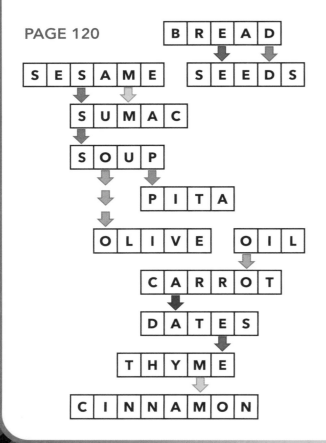

PAGES 122-123

| O | D | I | U | M | A | E |

I cry aloud to God, and He will hear me. In the day of my trouble, I seek the Lord; in the night my hand is stretched out without wearying; my soul refuses to be comforted. When I remember God, I moan; when I meditate, my spirit faints. You hold my eyelids open; I am so troubled that I cannot speak. I consider the days of old, the years long ago. I said, "Let me remember my song in the night; let me meditate in my heart." PSALM 77:1-6 ESV

PAGE 124

F3	D5	A5
B6	B4	D2
F7	B1	D5

PAGES 126-127

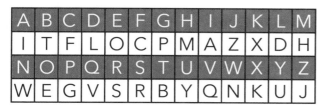

A	B	C	D	E	F	G	H	I	J	K	L	M
I	T	F	L	O	C	P	M	A	Z	X	D	H
N	O	P	Q	R	S	T	U	V	W	X	Y	Z
W	E	G	V	S	R	B	Y	Q	N	K	U	J

If you had faith the size of a grain of mustard seed, you could say to a mulberry tree, "Be uprooted and planted in the sea," and it would obey you.

PAGE 129

"If you have faith like a grain of mustard seed, you could say to a mountain, "Move from here to there," and it will move, and nothing will be impossible for you.

PAGES 130-131

A	B	C	D	E	F	G	H	I	J	K	L	M
3	15	9	19	2	13	21	6	10	23	16	1	8
N	O	P	Q	R	S	T	U	V	W	X	Y	Z
18	5	11	14	12	7	4	22	17	20	26	25	24

It's not about size. It's about who your faith is in. If you are secure in your faith in God, trusting in his promises, choosing his will for your life instead of your own, tiny sized faith is enough.

PAGES 132-133

SEED, HEED, HELD, HOLD, HOLE, HOPE

HOPE, HOSE, HOST, POST, PEST, BEST, BEAT, HEAT, HEAL

PAGES 134-135

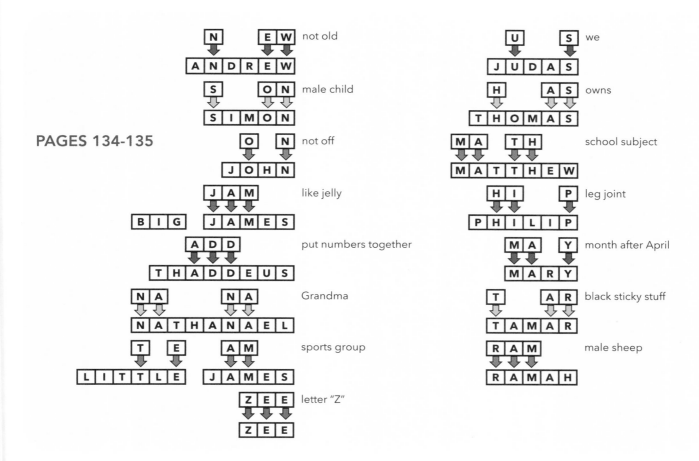

WATER
RATE, TARE, TEAR, WARE, WART, WEAR
ARE, ART, ATE, AWE, EAR, EAT, ERA, RAT, RAW, TAR, TEA, WAR, WET
AT, AW, ER, EW, WE

PAGE 147

"Come to me all who labor and are heavy laden, and I will give you rest. Take my yoke upon you, and learn from me, for I am gentle and lowly in heart, and you will find rest for your souls. For my yoke is easy, and my burden is light!"

PAGE 148
Don't let me go!

PAGES 136-137
A man had two sons. He went to the first and said, "Son, go and work in the vineyard today." And he answered, "I will not." But afterward he changed his mind and went. The man went to the other son and said the same. And he answered, "I will go, sir." But he did not go.

Which of the two did the will of the father?

PAGE 139
12 baskets

PAGE 142
1. C, D
2. G, H
3. A, B
4. F, E

PAGE 144
STORMY
STORM, STORY
MOST, ROSY, ROTS, SORT, TOYS
ROT, SOY, STY, TOY, TRY
MY, OR, SO, TO